Scenarios for ESL Standards-Based Assessment

Teachers of English to Speakers of Other Languages, Inc.

Typeset in Giovanni and Novarese
by Capitol Communication Systems, Inc., Crofton, Maryland USA
Printed by Kirby Lithographic Company, Inc., Arlington, Virginia USA

Teachers of English to Speakers of Other Languages, Inc.
700 South Washington Street, Suite 200
Alexandria, VA 22314 USA
Tel. 703-836-0774 • Fax 703-836-7864 • E-mail tesol@tesol.org • http://www.tesol.org/

Assessment Team:
Anne Katz, Chair, ARC Associates
Fred Genesee, McGill University
Margo Gottlieb, Illinois Resource Center
Margaret Malone, Center for Applied Linguistics

Scenario Writers:
Nancy Clair
Jennifer Delett
Mary Fox
Sandra Fradd
Margo Gottlieb
Gary Hargett
Anne Katz
Deborah Liston-Romero
Margaret Malone
Janet Orr
Maggie Rosen
Sue Wallace

Additional Members of ESL Standards
and Assessment Project:
Nancy Cloud, Rhode Island College
Emily Gómez, Center for Applied Linguistics
Else Hamayan, Illinois Resource Center
Sarah Hudelson, Arizona State University
Jean Ramirez, San Francisco Unified School District
Deborah Short, Project Director, Center for Applied Linguistics

TESOL Board Liaisons:
Natalie Kuhlman, San Diego State University
Adelaide Parsons, Southeast Missouri State University
Charles S. Amorosino, Jr., Executive Director, TESOL

Director of Communications and Marketing: Helen Kornblum
Managing Editor: Marilyn Kupetz
Copy Editor: Marcella Fecteau Weiner
Additional Reader: Marcia Annis
Cover Design: Ann Kammerer

ISBN 0-939791-90-0

Library of Congress Catalogue No. 2001 131316

Dedication

To J. Michael O'Malley, a consummate professional, whose contribution to the field of assessment and language minority education is immeasurable.

Table of Contents

Part 3: Understanding and Using Assessment Data

Preface

ESL Standards for Pre-K–12 Students (TESOL, 1997) has given an important tool to ESL professionals and others in the educational community interested in creating effective programs for linguistically and culturally diverse students. The ESL standards have become a starting point for necessary discussions about how best to serve the needs of our students by building rich curricula and designing more effective instruction—key components of useful education programs. *Scenarios for ESL Standards-Based Assessment* adds another and necessary component to that discussion: assessment. It presents an assessment process for measuring students' progress in attaining ESL standards and a series of classroom-based scenarios illustrating how to weave the assessment process into ongoing instruction.

Like *ESL Standards, Scenarios for ESL Standards-Based Assessment* is designed as part of the larger ESL Standards and Assessment Project underwritten by TESOL. A booklet conceptualizing the framework for assessment, entitled *Managing the Assessment Process: A Framework for Measuring Student Attainment of the ESL Standards* (*MAP*), was published by TESOL in 1998 as Professional Paper No. 5. *MAP* provides educators with a conceptual model for assessment, principles to guide assessment of ESOL students, and suggestions for approaches to implement this model. *MAP* has been incorporated into this book as the section entitled "Part 1: Framework for Assessment" and presents the theoretical framework for assessment exemplified in the scenarios. Other companion pieces in this project include *Training Others to Use the ESL Standards: A Professional Development Manual,* for teacher trainers; *Implementing the Pre-K–12 ESL Standards Through Teacher Education,* for teacher training courses; *Integrating the ESL Standards Into Classroom Practice,* a four-volume series of curriculum guides, for classroom teachers; *The Administrator's Guide to the ESL Standards*; and *A Parent's Guide to TESOL's ESL Standards for Pre-K–12 Students.*

This book is closely aligned with *ESL Standards for Pre-K–12 Students.* Our scenarios are based on the vignettes found in *ESL Standards.* Where the standards vignettes present a snapshot of standards-based instruction, these scenarios represent classroom videos, so to speak. The scenarios illustrate how assessment can be integrated with instructional activities over an extended period of time. The strength of both books comes from the extensive involvement of ESL professionals in developing and writing the vignettes and scenarios. We are grateful to everyone who participated in this process. Their experience contributed to the books' authenticity.

Anne Katz (Chair), ARC Associates
Fred Genesee, McGill University
Margo Gottlieb, Illinois Resource Center
Margaret Malone, Center for Applied Linguistics

Introduction

In this book, we provide a variety of resources to assist teachers in incorporating assessment into a standards-referenced curriculum. We have organized these resources into the following sections.

Tips for Using This Book

We realize that for many people, reading a book on assessment may be intimidating. Most of us envision ourselves as proficient in instruction but less confident in assessment. In this section, we offer 10 tips to consider when delving into this book so that your effort is productive.

Part 1: Framework for Assessment

This section sets out the theoretical framework shaping our approach to assessment. It includes an overview of assessment, key terms useful for understanding the framework, a conceptual model of assessment, principles highlighting the role of linguistic and cultural diversity in the assessment process, a discussion of the role of purpose and audience in designing assessment plans, and approaches to and uses for assessment.

Part 2: Assessment Scenarios

In this section, the framework for assessment is translated into practice in the day-to-day business of classrooms serving ESOL students. The scenarios are organized by ESL goal and standard, progressing from Goal 1, Standard 1, to Goal 3, Standard 3. As in the ESL standards vignettes, classroom contexts vary across grade levels and program design. We acknowledge, however, that there are more contexts present in school systems across the United States than are represented in the scenarios. We trust in your expertise as TESOL professionals to take the ideas illustrated in this book and make them fit your situation. In several places, we have emphasized the need for professional development to assist in the systematic implementation of a standards-based assessment process. Such professional development can be very useful in creating a smoother match between suggested practice and real-life classrooms. To assist in the implementation process, this section of the book ends with "A Plan for Standards-Based Instruction and Assessment."

This section also includes an index to offer readers quicker access to areas of interest in the scenarios. The index lists specific topics and where they can be located within specific scenarios. (Another index, at the end of Part 3, provides a list of the assessment forms used in the scenarios along with page numbers and grade levels.)

Part 3: Understanding and Using Assessment Data

Throughout this book, we emphasize the need for systematicity in implementing an assessment system. Once information is collected, we also focus on determining what it may mean for various stakeholders. This section provides suggestions for setting up assessment systems and for understanding the data collected in terms of targeted performance levels.

As you look through this book, you will note that we have not tried to adhere rigorously to a set format. The variation across the scenarios reflects different writers and different ways of organizing classroom instruction and assessment. We purposely retained this variation to emphasize that the scenarios are not templates but rather are starting points for considering ways to incorporate standards-referenced assessment into classrooms.

We also believe multiple measures can provide the kind of sound information that will help educators make better decisions about instruction. In charting student progress toward attaining specific standards, the teachers in our scenarios employ a range of assessment tools. Please do not feel daunted or overwhelmed by all of the strategies used, for our intent is merely to show the rich possibilities as you consider how to implement a decision-making assessment process.

One last, but important, caveat: Throughout the scenarios we have used *ESL Standards* as our starting point for designing lessons. Nearly all of the scenarios are based on the classroom vignettes taken from *ESL Standards*. Yet we know that many districts modify national standards to reflect state standards and to fit local contexts. Please remember that our use of the national standards reflects our intent to show how standards can be used as the reference point for designing instruction and assessment. We assume that your own implementation efforts will utilize locally developed or adapted ESL standards appropriate for the ESOL learners in your classrooms.

Tips for Using This Book

We have put together a list of tips for using this book because we know that so much information can be overwhelming. We hope these tips make the book more useful to you as you look for ways to apply new ideas for instruction and assessment.

Tip 1: These are suggestions.

One way to think of this book is as a grocery list rather than a recipe book. Its purpose is not to provide you with a step-by-step recipe of how to assess your students. Your situation is probably not identical to any teacher's classroom in the scenarios, and you cannot expect to do everything exemplified in the scenarios. Instead, you can focus on ways to apply these ideas to your own setting.

Tip 2: Do not let all the information overwhelm you.

This book is very dense and may seem overwhelming. For example, the assessment principles on pages 7–10 are comprehensive. They include many issues that may go beyond one teacher's power to shape day-to-day assessment practices. The principles are really goals to work toward—for you as a teacher and for your program. The scenarios offer ideas for you to consider. They are not a mandate for practice.

Tip 3: Take what works.

Our job as teaching professionals is to take input and ideas and make them fit our situations. Some approaches will work for you; others will not. When you read through this book, try to keep an open mind. Try some new approaches and see which ones work best.

Tip 4: Read the whole scenario.

It is a good idea to read the whole scenario, even if it does not seem to apply to your group of students. The connections and discussion sections talk about different applications or critiques of the assessment approaches. This is a good place to get ideas that might apply to your setting.

Tip 5: Instruction and assessment are a matched pair.

This book shows different ways to align ESL instruction with classroom assessments. The sample progress indicators in each scenario show the salient points of language instruction that must be assessed to show student progress. It is also important to select assessment approaches that are appropriate for the content of instruction that will provide relevant information to students and teachers alike.

Tip 6: Variety is important.

The scenarios are based on the vignettes presented in *ESL Standards for Pre-K–12 Students* (TESOL, 1997). The scenarios expand on the vignettes and show a variety of approaches to assessment. Any standard can be assessed in many different ways. Whereas you should not rely on only one method of assessment to assess a standard, you also do not have to use all the approaches outlined in this book. We hope that the scenarios provide examples of some ways to assess the standards and that you can find some new ideas.

Tip 7: Collecting versus recording information can sometimes overlap.

Traditional tests are administered at one point in time (collecting information), and the grades are later entered in the teacher's grade book (recording information). By contrast, many authentic assessments, such as portfolios, collect and record information almost simultaneously, and it may be hard to distinguish between the two steps. For a clear-cut example of the distinction between collecting and recording, see the scenario for Goal 2, Standard 2, Grades 4–8. For an example of the ambiguity that may arise in portfolio assessment, see the scenario for Goal 3, Standard 1.

Tip 8: Learning strategies are not used uniformly.

In these scenarios, learning strategies are goals that are emphasized just as they are in the ESL standards. However, not every school focuses on learning strategies in instruction, and they are often difficult to assess. Because the scenarios show the realm of possibilities in the ESL classroom, we hope that the scenarios on learning strategies will give you new ideas for classroom approaches.

Tip 9: Use this book for professional development.

This book, along with *ESL Standards*, can be used in conjunction with your school's or district's program for ESL and other classroom teachers. Working through this book with your colleagues will allow you to explore new ways to approach instruction and assessment. It may also help you and your colleagues find better ways to collaborate in providing services to ESOL students.

Tip 10: Enjoy it!

This is your book. Many teachers worked to make it accessible for you. The most important part of the book is its usability for teachers. If you can find new and useful approaches to assessment, then the book is a success.

List of ESL Standards

Goal 1: To Use English to Communicate in Social Settings

Standard 1:   Students will use English to participate in social interaction.

Standard 2:   Students will interact in, through, and with spoken and written English for personal expression and enjoyment.

Standard 3:   Students will use learning strategies to extend their communicative competence.

Goal 2: To Use English to Achieve Academically in All Content Areas

Standard 1:   Students will use English to interact in the classroom.

Standard 2:   Students will use English to obtain, process, construct, and provide subject matter information in spoken and written form.

Standard 3:   Students will use appropriate learning strategies to construct and apply academic knowledge.

Goal 3: To Use English in Socially and Culturally Appropriate Ways

Standard 1:   Students will use the appropriate language variety, register, and genre according to audience, purpose, and setting.

Standard 2:   Students will use nonverbal communication appropriate to audience, purpose, and setting.

Standard 3:   Students will use appropriate learning strategies to extend their sociolinguistic and sociocultural competence. (TESOL, 1997, pp. 9–10)

Part 1: Framework for Assessment

Framework for Assessment

Overview

"Part 1: Framework for Assessment"[1] provides a window into the complexities of assessment and suggests some ways to think about assessing ESOL students.[2] Its primary audience is teachers who provide direct services to ESOL students in a variety of pre-K–12 settings, including ESL teachers, bilingual teachers, content-area teachers, and teachers of students with special needs and talents.[3] However, all stakeholders in the assessment process, including students, parents, principals, district and state administrators as well as national policy makers, will find this document helpful for defining their roles in the assessment process.

This section offers a general description of assessment and some considerations in the assessment of ESOL students. Figure 1.1 illustrates the linkages among instruction, assessment, and *ESL Standards for Pre-K–12 Students* within the context of teaching and learning. The ESL standards should serve as the foundation for planning lessons, designing instructional assessment tasks, or selecting or developing assessments that further student learning.

By focusing on assessment, we may seem to be slighting what we as teachers take to be our primary responsibility—that of planning and implementing instruction. As Figure 1.2 illustrates, however, we see assessment as one component in a system focused on the delivery of high-quality educational experiences for learners.

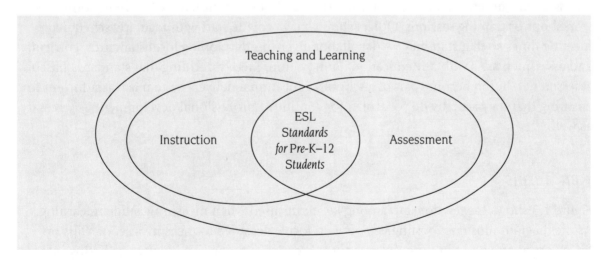

FIGURE 1.1 THE CONTEXT FOR INSTRUCTION AND ASSESSMENT FOR ESOL STUDENTS

[1] An earlier version of this section was originally published by TESOL in 1998 as *Managing the Assessment Process: A Framework for Measuring Student Attainment of the ESL Standards* (Professional Paper 5).

[2] *ESOL* stands for "English to speakers of other languages." The term refers to learners who are in the process of acquiring English as an additional language.

[3] Because we have defined the primary audience as teachers, much of the text uses the terms *teachers* or *educators* when describing how to apply the assessment process. However, we recognize that other audiences may be involved in instituting this process as well.

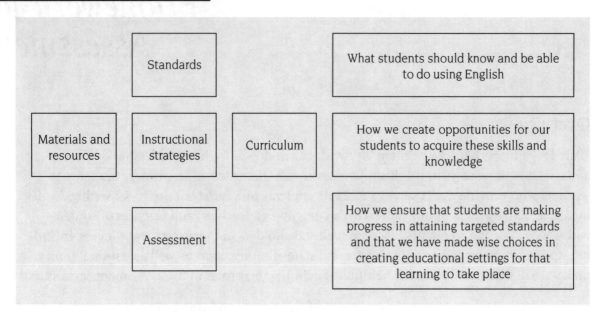

FIGURE 1.2 DELIVERING HIGH-QUALITY EDUCATIONAL EXPERIENCES

Need for Professional Development

Many of the practices illustrated throughout this book reflect what some teachers do on a regular basis in their classrooms, but many other teachers have not had exposure to or training in sound assessment practices. Schools and districts that seek to implement standards-based reform will need to support staff in learning and developing the skills necessary for this effort. Some of this professional development may come in the form of workshops or training sessions. Other schools may provide staff with regularly scheduled meeting times so that staff may work collaboratively on developing local standards, curricula, and assessments. As with any educational innovation, merely deciding that standards-based assessments should become part of a school's educational delivery system is not sufficient for ensuring that they actually do so. A plan for continued professional development is necessary as well.

Key Terms

Figure 1.3 shows the relationship among key terms used when measuring student learning. As the diagram illustrates, testing is narrow in focus, designed to measure a set of skills or behaviors at one point in time. Assessment is broader in scope and involves gathering information over a period of time. This information might include formal tests, classroom observations, student self-assessments, or data from other sources. The focus of this book is classroom assessment that measures student performance. Evaluation is broadest in scope and refers to assessment data that have been analyzed to make judgments or draw inferences about students and educational programs.

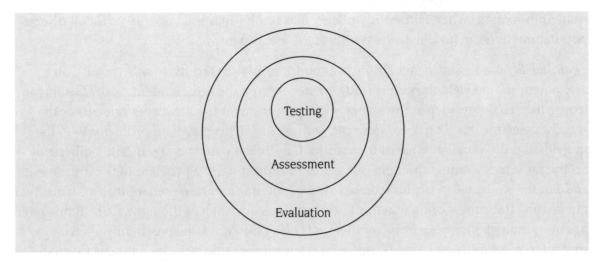

FIGURE 1.3 DISTINCTION AMONG TESTING, ASSESSMENT, AND EVALUATION

Classroom assessments are interwoven into instruction, often created and delivered by ESL/bilingual teachers. Large-scale assessments are planned and conducted at the district, state, or national levels and are often considered high-stakes assessments because they can result in consequences for students, teachers, or schools. For example, in some states, high school graduation depends on passing a large-scale assessment. The framework for large-scale assessment should include ESOL students and special needs students, thus reducing the need for accommodations[4] and modifications once the assessment has been adopted. The principles and discussions throughout this book refer to both large-scale and classroom assessment, unless specified otherwise.

Additional terms to describe assessments and the assessment process include *fairness, reliability, validity,* and *usefulness.* These terms are defined here and are always used with these technical definitions.

Fairness refers to the assessment's equity throughout the assessment process. Fairness implies equal access to and opportunities for learning for all students, particularly with regard to students' diverse linguistic, cultural, and educational backgrounds. For example, in planning assessments, fairness should be reflected in the selection of the ESL standards and their alignment with the purposes for assessment. When collecting information, identifying background information about students and looking at the purposes of programmatic assessment are important in establishing fairness. When analyzing and interpreting information, the information collected must be put into context with regard to the ESOL population. Finally, when reporting the results, all contextual features, including the diverse backgrounds of students, parents, and other stakeholders, must be considered before deciding how to

---

[4] *Accommodations* is the term most commonly associated with changes made in testing formats and conditions when assessing special needs students. Accommodations include extended time, large print for visually impaired students, and the reading of text for students with learning differences. Accommodations for special needs students must be specified in each student's individualized educational plan (IEP). Recently, however, the term accommodations has been used in large-scale assessment of ESOL students.

share information. When fairness is violated, bias results. Bias is a major issue for all diverse populations and can invalidate the results of the assessment.

Reliability is an assessment's ability to produce consistent results. In other words, an assessment should yield the same results, or scores, from the same student. Many factors can jeopardize reliability, such as the accuracy of the instrument used to assess students or the way the assessment is scored. For example, some assessments may have problems with the individual tasks a student is asked to perform. If a student performs significantly differently on the same task within a short period of time, it is most likely a problem of the instrument and not the student. Raters who score an assessment may also cause reliability problems. Two raters using the same scoring system should give the same student the same score. If one rater has been trained differently from another, or is using the criteria inconsistently, then a student may get different scores by different raters on the same task. Such threats to reliability are not the fault of the instrument but of the raters.[5]

Validity refers to the assessment's match between the information collected and its specified purpose(s). For example, an oral proficiency assessment that relies on students writing an essay would not be a valid assessment instrument. In addition, a standardized measure that has been designed and normed on native-English-speaking students is not a valid tool for ESOL students. Validity is also dependent on reliability. If an instrument is not reliable, it cannot be valid. Validity is the responsibility of both test developer and test user. In many of the scenarios, we have demonstrated how to align standards-based sample progress indicators (SPIs) with instructional activities and assessments to ensure greater validity. See, for example, Figure 2.23 in the scenario for Goal 2, Standard 2, Grades 4–8.

Finally, an assessment's *usefulness* is crucial. Usefulness is an assessment's ability to meet the needs of its users while providing the maximum amount of reliability and validity. Usefulness includes the cost, both for money and for time, and management in the use or administration of the assessment.

A Conceptual Model for Assessment

Teachers, administrators, and policy makers make numerous decisions every day that have an impact on the education of ESOL students. For example, teachers make decisions about the appropriateness of instructional plans for individual students with special needs or talents, administrators make decisions about the eligibility and placement of new students, and policy makers make decisions about the adoption and implementation of new programs. Assessment supports the process of making these kinds of decisions. It provides the information necessary to guide educators in determining students' progress in attaining the language competencies specified in *ESL Standards for Pre-K–12 Students* (TESOL, 1997). The assessment process includes planning, collecting and recording, analyzing and interpreting, and using relevant information for decision making and reporting. Figure 1.4 illustrates this dynamic and cyclical process.

---

[5] For further discussion, see "Part 3: Understanding and Using Assessment Data."

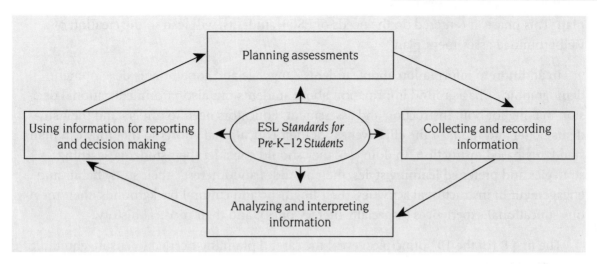

FIGURE 1.4 THE ASSESSMENT PROCESS

As illustrated, assessment is a purposeful, multiphased, systematic, and ongoing process. When ESOL students are represented in the pre-K–12 student population, several factors must be considered in assessment design. First, linguistic and cultural characteristics need to be taken into account when formulating the assessment plan. The assessment design should also build on the developmental nature of language acquisition for all students, acknowledging as well the additional demands facing ESOL learners. ESOL learners have had access to different cultural and academic language experiences. As a result, it may take such students longer than others to learn English. This developmental perspective, illustrated in Figure 1.5, underlies any assessment process that claims to measure student learning over time.

Principles of Assessment

In this section, principles highlighting the role of linguistic and cultural diversity are embedded within the different phases of the assessment process. These principles support educators in making equitable decisions for ESOL students.

PLANNING ASSESSMENTS

Planning is perhaps the most crucial part of the assessment process because it clarifies purposes, defines stakeholders, identifies assessment approaches, and establishes a management

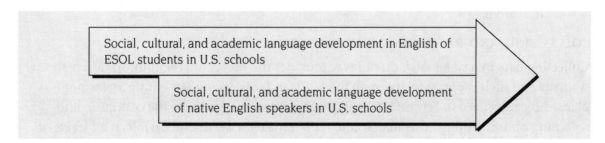

FIGURE 1.5 PATHWAY TO LANGUAGE DEVELOPMENT OF PRE-K–12 STUDENTS

plan. This phase, if centered on the needs of ESOL students, will lead to the creation of a well-grounded assessment plan.

In addition to information about students' language and content-area development, demographic or background information about students can also inform educational decision making for both instruction and assessment. Educators need to understand their students better and monitor the effectiveness of their educational efforts so that they can plan standards-based instruction. In doing so, they should consider their students' learning strategies and preferred learning styles, their attitudes and interests, their study habits and engagement in instructional activities, their linguistic and cultural backgrounds, their previous educational experiences (especially literacy ones), and their medical history.

The first 8 (of the 19) principles reveal the careful planning needed to ensure equitable assessment practices.

1. The students' ages, levels of proficiency and academic achievement in first and second languages, learning styles, educational continuity inside and outside the United States, and amount of time receiving ESL/bilingual support provide the background information for assessment.

2. Assessments draw on the social, cultural, and academic experiences of ESOL learners.

3. Assessments are based on current educational research, especially in the areas of first and second language acquisition.

4. Assessments allow ESOL students to demonstrate complex learning in contextualized ways, such as through the use of real objects or graphics (e.g., pictures, charts, tables, diagrams, photographs, graphic organizers).

5. Classroom assessments mirror the language(s) and content of instruction and instructional practices.

6. Classroom assessments enable students to demonstrate their learning in multiple ways from multiple perspectives, thus serving as learning experiences themselves.

7. Classroom assessments, which may be a part of thematic projects, promote student involvement and reflection on learning and require students to use a variety of learning strategies and resources.

8. Assessment documents or rubrics represent the full range of student performance and are designed with a set of clearly defined criteria against which the standards are measured.

COLLECTING AND RECORDING INFORMATION

Collecting data in a systematic, careful way provides the most consistent information about students and their progress in attaining the ESL standards. In implementing assessment plans, educators need to rely on a management system to coordinate the collection and recording of information. This management plan makes assessment feasible at all levels of implementation (e.g., classroom, program, school, district, state, national). Prior to gathering information, teachers should consider how they will use and analyze data. Consistency also needs to be maintained in recording assessment information. The next four principles provide guidance on collection and record keeping.

9. Multiple types of assessment, including both criterion-referenced and norm-referenced measures, are used to form a composite picture of ESOL student performance over time.

10. Information from classroom assessment for monitoring student progress is gathered within the instructional cycle (i.e., lesson, theme, project, unit).

11. Assessments use multiple sources of information, including teachers, parents, and students themselves, to provide a clear picture of student performance.

12. Assessment data are collected and recorded systematically with a uniform set of procedures and guidelines for administration.

ANALYZING AND INTERPRETING ASSESSMENT INFORMATION

Analyzing and interpreting assessment information is the phase in which the information collected and recorded is examined according to the purposes established in the assessment plan. For example, if portfolio entries have been collected, the portfolio as a whole should be analyzed according to a scale or set of criteria. Some analyses may show that a student has reached a certain level of language proficiency or can perform tasks in class similar to ESOL or native-English-speaking peers. Analyses can also reflect the extent to which specific standards have been met. The next three principles address issues of analyzing assessment information.

13. Data are analyzed and interpreted in light of the particular characteristics that define ESOL students, such as those suggested in Principle 1.

14. Teachers need to be able to pair specified criteria or descriptors with samples of ESOL student work to gain a sense of the range of student performance.

15. English language assessments for ESOL students at the upper end of the proficiency continuum should be linked to the average performance of native-English-speaking peers to facilitate educational continuity and success.

USING INFORMATION FOR REPORTING AND DECISION MAKING

This final phase of the assessment process continues the collaboration of teachers with other stakeholders. For example, an individual student's portfolio may be shared with the parents, whereas a composite class or school portfolio may be shared with school and district officials. Such results allow stakeholders to make informed decisions, based on their original purposes for assessment, on issues such as student reclassification or program improvement. These final four principles relate to reporting and decision making.

16. Results from assessments are used to enhance instruction, improve student performance, and aid in educational decision making.

17. Results from assessments are understandable and useful to students and the greater educational community. Information is presented clearly and in the appropriate language(s).

18. Results from assessments are reported to stakeholders with reference to ESOL students' performance of designated standards.

19. Results are reported in a timely fashion to stakeholders (i.e., while information is still current and applicable), and all relevant information is compiled and considered before a decision is rendered.

These 19 principles should form the basis for a comprehensive professional development program in assessment for all teachers. A coordinated effort among teachers is necessary to have continuity of student data from year to year. When all teachers are vested in instruction and assessment practice, students will benefit.

Purposes of Assessment and Stakeholders' Involvement

Different members of the pre-K–12 educational community will assess attainment of ESL standards for different purposes. Figure 1.6 illustrates the range of stakeholders and purposes for collecting such assessment information. At the classroom level, for example, teachers might collect assessment information to determine whether students have mastered new material, using students' performances on classroom tasks as a guide for lesson planning. At the program level, coordinators may use the results of individual student assessment to place students in appropriate instructional settings.

Given the range of stakeholders and purposes, educators rely on a variety of assessment approaches to make informed decisions. Such decisions should result from collaboration among educators, such as principals, coordinators, and teachers working together to determine and implement student assessment practices. Approaches appropriate to one set of stakeholders and purposes, however, may not provide useful information in other educational settings. Every educator must judge the suitability of particular methods relative to specific purposes, students, settings, and audiences at different times during the course of instruction. Thus, it is important for all educators to understand the relative utility of multiple ways to collect and record information for assessing the attainment of the ESL standards.

Approaches to Assessment

This section discusses different approaches to assessment, along with some ways to record the results of these assessments. Some approaches include performance-based assessments; proficiency-based assessments; and commercially developed, nationally norm-referenced tests. There are many ways to collect and record information, including anecdotal records, checklists, rating scales, journals, and portfolios. No single approach to assessment or method of record keeping is satisfactory for all purposes and stakeholders. Instead, using multiple approaches and record-keeping methods can help demonstrate and document student progress thoroughly and accurately. Although assessment can occur in many settings, a great deal of it occurs in the ESL/bilingual classroom. Other settings, such as content-area

FIGURE 1.6 STAKEHOLDERS AND PURPOSES FOR ASSESSMENT AT EACH LEVEL OF IMPLEMENTATION

Level of Implementation	Stakeholders	Purposes
Classroom	• students • parents • teachers	• allow students to assess their own progress • monitor students' progress toward attainment of ESL standards • provide ongoing diagnostic information • create partnerships that foster communication among parents, students, and teachers • plan and improve instruction
Program	• teachers • coordinators/directors • principals • counselors	• screen, place, and transition students in the program • monitor the program's progress toward student attainment of ESL standards • document student learning • improve program effectiveness
School/district	• principals • assistant superintendents • superintendents • parent advisory committees	• ascertain the extent to which standards have been met • guide professional development of teachers • determine effectiveness of teaching and learning • review policy based on assessment/evaluation information
State	• superintendents • state boards of education • business community • legislatures	• be accountable for student learning based on attainment of standards • report summary information • create linkages with schools/districts • act on summary information and trend data
National	• Office for Civil Rights • U.S. Department of Education • Congress	• ensure equitable educational opportunities • enforce court decisions regarding ESOL students

Note. From "A Peek Into Portfolio Practices" (pp. 23–36), by M. Gottlieb. In A. Huhta, V. Kohonen, L. Kurki-Suonio, & S. Luoma (Eds.), *Current Developments and Alternatives in Language Assessments: Proceedings of LTRC 96*, 1997, Jyvaskyla, Finland: University of Jyvaskyla. Adapted with permission.

classrooms, the lunchroom, the school yard, and the home, can be excellent sources of information on students.

In deciding which assessment(s) to use in an instructional program, it is helpful to choose the type or types of assessment necessary for the instructional setting and purpose. There are several different ways to distinguish among types of assessment: criterion-referenced versus norm-referenced, language proficiency versus academic achievement, and direct performance versus indirect performance. Figure 1.7 briefly outlines the differences among these types of assessment.

Figure 1.7 Different Types of Assessment

Criterion-referenced	Norm-referenced
Compares student performances against a set of predefined criteria. In standards-based assessment, a type of criterion-referenced assessment, the standard serves as the criterion. Can be used in the classroom to measure student progress in learning an instructional objective, when the criteria are developed by teachers; throughout a school, when the criteria are school based; or on a statewide test, when the criteria are developed by the state.	Provides information on how students perform with respect to their peers around the country. On these kinds of tests, students are ranked against each other. May be used to show how students have progressed relative to similar populations at different levels of implementation.
Language proficiency	**Academic achievement**
Captures a student's holistic ability in a language, generally showing the extent to which a student has acquired a second language. It can be used to ascertain a student's global proficiency in the areas of listening, speaking, reading, and writing.	Measures a student's mastery of curricular material. The results of an achievement test could be used to measure a student's progress in relation to the instructional content.
Direct performance	**Indirect performance**
Requires the student to show specified knowledge through demonstration. For example, a direct assessment of oral proficiency requires a student to speak.	Relies on a less authentic means of capturing knowledge. For example, a vocabulary test does not directly assess reading, but it does assess a component of reading. In addition, an indirect assessment may be descriptive of the way in which the data are used, such as relying on a written transcript for oral language.

In addition to assessment results collected in ESL/bilingual classrooms, educational decision making calls for many different kinds of information about students. This information may come from different sources. For example, content-area teachers can collaborate with ESL or bilingual teachers to discuss student progress as evidenced by their in-class performance or by test results, students can work on peer and self-assessment, and parents can share information with teachers during parent/teacher conferences. In addition, this information can contribute to the creation and revision of special needs students' individualized education plans (IEPs). The results can inform the ESL/bilingual teacher of a student's ability to use English in socially and culturally appropriate ways.

Figure 1.8 identifies some activities associated with the whole assessment process. When planning assessments, teachers need to define their purposes and audiences. In the case of performance assessments, the type of performance or task would be chosen and the rating scale and criteria would be reviewed. In the case of a proficiency assessment, a preexisting assessment with valid, reliable criteria for rating would be selected. Finally, in considering a commercially developed, nationally norm-referenced test, its purpose, along with the test's appropriateness for a specific group of students, would be considered. To ensure the success of the assessment plan, teachers and others involved in assessment should receive the professional development and support needed for implementation throughout the assessment process.

The collection and recording of information relies on a variety of record-keeping methods. In addition to the relatively straightforward administration of a standardized test according to the designated directions, teachers can use student journals, anecdotal records of observations, portfolios, and checklists of students' performances. When students are engaged in an instructional activity or task that will be assessed, such as a science experiment, a social studies demonstration, or a storytelling, teachers need to have a clear set of criteria to score or interpret students' performance. These criteria or descriptors are often defined in a form called a rubric. Together, the rubric and student performance constitute the assessment.

Rubrics usually take the form of holistic scales, checklists, rating scales, or matrices. At the classroom level, rubrics may be task or project specific; at a school, district, or state level, the criteria are more generalized and specifically aligned to standards. Classroom rubrics should be designed by the team of teachers who plan to use them; school or program rubrics should be selected and modified to serve in assessing the work of the specific group of students.

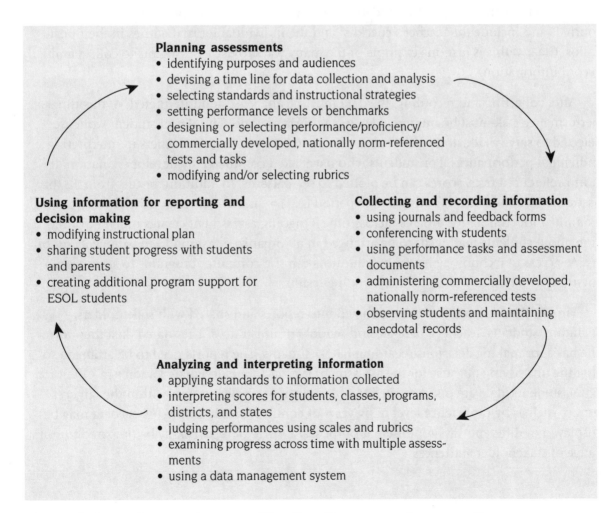

Planning assessments
- identifying purposes and audiences
- devising a time line for data collection and analysis
- selecting standards and instructional strategies
- setting performance levels or benchmarks
- designing or selecting performance/proficiency/ commercially developed, nationally norm-referenced tests and tasks
- modifying and/or selecting rubrics

Using information for reporting and decision making
- modifying instructional plan
- sharing student progress with students and parents
- creating additional program support for ESOL students

Collecting and recording information
- using journals and feedback forms
- conferencing with students
- using performance tasks and assessment documents
- administering commercially developed, nationally norm-referenced tests
- observing students and maintaining anecdotal records

Analyzing and interpreting information
- applying standards to information collected
- interpreting scores for students, classes, programs, districts, and states
- judging performances using scales and rubrics
- examining progress across time with multiple assessments
- using a data management system

FIGURE 1.8 SAMPLE ACTIVITIES ASSOCIATED WITH EACH PHASE OF THE ASSESSMENT PROCESS

After designing a rubric, the members of the rubric development team should design and implement a system for training their colleagues to use the rubric. It is important for teachers to develop a common way of applying the rubric to student work to maintain the reliability of the rubric. If the rubric is applied in different ways by different teachers, then the rubric is unreliable.

When the team of teachers develops a writing rubric, for example, it should work to base benchmarks on student writing samples to exemplify each level of the rubric. Then, the team can share the rubric and the benchmark samples with colleagues. If several teachers rate the same student and arrive at the same result, then the rubric is considered reliable. It is not necessary for every student paper to be rated by several different teachers; however, it is important for at least two teachers to rate a common set of writing samples to demonstrate the rubric's reliability.

If a teacher gives a standardized test to the class, each student's score on the test is one piece of information. The teacher could also ask the students to reflect on the experience in their journals and discuss their reflections at a conference, adding two more data sources. In the case of a performance assessment, the teacher might use a checklist to assess the students' abilities to perform the task. The students might also reflect on this performance in their journals and include the teacher's checklist and the individual journal entries in their portfolios. Clearly, this is just one example of the many ways to use assessments to collect and record information.

After collecting and recording, the data must be analyzed and interpreted. At this time, a performance task must be interpreted using a rubric or scale. Samples of student work are selected to serve as illustrations of rubrics and criteria and to guide teachers in interpreting individual performances. For students who have taken commercially developed, nationally norm-referenced tests, scores can be plotted to see patterns. In addition, results from all the assessments administered during a time period (e.g., a quarter, semester, school year) can be examined for cumulative progress across time. Ongoing assessment creates much information about students that needs to be arranged in an organized fashion to maximize its usability. As access to technology increases, educators can use computer programs to store assessment information as well as to analyze some results.

Finally, the analyzed data are organized into reports and shared with stakeholders, including students, teachers, parents, and school administrators. The shared data then form the basis for making decisions regarding ESOL students. The reports need to be arranged so that the underlying purpose for the assessment is clear to the designated audience. Often for ESOL students, data are disaggregated to reflect distinct smaller groups within the larger group, such as by proficiency level or by years of continuous education. Just as data may be displayed in different ways for different purposes, a range of reports may be prepared to suit a range of stakeholder audiences.

General Uses for Assessment Results

Assessment data can have several overarching uses:

- Assessment is useful for the creation of effective learning environments that promote nativelike levels of English language proficiency and appropriate grade-level academic achievement among ESOL students. Assessment results can assist teachers in modifying their instructional plans to better meet the needs of their students. Information gained from assessment can also help students identify their accomplishments and areas for further development. Assessment is an essential part of creating effective learning environments because it provides the information critical for the numerous day-to-day and high-stakes decisions made about ESOL students and their instruction.

- Assessment is an important component of accountability for all educators and policy makers who work with or are involved in the education of ESOL students. Assessment results can assist teachers, school administrators, district personnel, and policy makers to determine the appropriateness and effectiveness of their educational policies and programs for ESOL students. The results of properly designed assessments can guide educational professionals who work in ESL classrooms, the whole school, or the district to create effective learning environments for ESOL students by (a) extending their understanding of ESOL students and their learning needs; (b) identifying educational policies, plans, and practices that are successful with ESOL students; and (c) demonstrating whether ESOL students have been given full access to challenging instruction and a full and appropriate range of educational opportunities, including experiences with new technologies and pedagogies.

- If the results of ESL assessment are shared openly and regularly with ESOL students and others, then these assessments can facilitate partnerships and linkages with students, parents, communities, and schools. Effective education for ESOL students requires that ESOL students and their parents are equal partners with fully proficient English-speaking students, parents, and teachers in managing schools.

Summary

Although general principles of good educational practice can serve all students, including linguistically and culturally diverse students, this book describes specific principles that will lead to equitable educational practice, specifically in assessment, for ESOL students. It also underscores the important linkages between instruction and assessment and stakeholders involved in the process.

Assessment is an essential component of effective education practices because it can indicate students' social, cultural, and academic accomplishments as well as their needs. Assessment provides information necessary for educators to make sound educational decisions. Assessment grows out of a recognition of the educational context; it is tied to the needs and characteristics of students being assessed, to the competencies of the teachers administering the assessments, and to the accountability demands of the larger institutional contexts within which students and teachers operate. Most important, assessment must be equitable; it must take into account both the ways in which assessment tools are designed and the ways in which they are used. As the National Commission on Testing and Public Policy (1977) notes, assessments must change "from a gatekeeper to a gateway" (p. 1).

Part 2: Assessment Scenarios

Assessment Scenarios

Overview

The scenarios are built around a series of assessment activities and tasks that are embedded in instruction. Classroom assessment consists of instructional activities and tasks that require students to demonstrate learning in direct ways, such as constructing a model, creating a product, or conducting an experiment, and the related forms of documentation or scoring guides needed, such as anecdotal records, checklists, rating scales, or holistic rubrics. Examples of peer or student self-assessment are included to provide richer profiles of ESOL student performance and to encourage ESOL students to be active participants in learning.

What differentiates classroom assessment from traditional assessment or testing is its open-ended nature. In this book, we include assessment activities and tasks within the scenarios that are performance based and involve nonverbal and verbal interaction as well as oral and written communication. The classroom assessments described in the scenarios share several features. They

- build on ESL standards and sample progress indicators

- trigger ESOL students' higher level thinking

- encourage the exploration of new ideas and concepts by students as well as teachers

- present multiple avenues to reach solutions, and ultimately, to attain the ESL standards

The scenarios, modeled on the vignettes in *ESL Standards for Pre-K–12 Students* (TESOL, 1997), include a variety of classroom backgrounds. We changed the backgrounds of the students in some scenarios from the original vignettes. We tried to make sure that scenarios include students from backgrounds that match as closely as possible the diversity of ESOL students in the United States. We include students with limited formal schooling and migrant students, teachers with dual language skills and ESOL certification, and teachers with limited experience with ESOL students. Although we show a representation of the rich range of first languages of students, it was, of course, impossible to include all the language backgrounds currently represented in U.S. schools.

Goal 2, Standard 2, addresses how we assess the attainment of content-area skills and concepts. Because this goal and standard provide a window into student progress on the academic content standards of their school districts, we developed four scenarios for this goal and standard across grade clusters. There is one for pre-K–3, one for 4–8, and two for 9–12. The first 9–12 scenario describes a classroom setting for ESOL students highly proficient in English; the second one shows how the same class could be adjusted for the needs of less proficient students.

Organization of the Scenarios

The assessment scenarios are framed around the three ESL goals and nine standards for social, academic, and cultural language competence for ESOL students. The scenarios are sequenced by goal and standard number and reflect a range of grade clusters. Figure 2.1 shows the organization of the scenarios.

All scenarios follow the same basic format. However, there is a great deal of individual variation within the scenarios to reflect a range of educational experiences and backgrounds.

GOAL AND STANDARD

All scenarios begin with the goal and standard addressed in the scenario, listed at the top of the page.

SAMPLE PROGRESS INDICATORS

Next, we list the sample progress indicators (SPIs) appropriate for assessing the goal and standard addressed in the scenario. The SPIs are assessable, observable behaviors related to the instructional unit. Because assessment is the focus of the scenarios, the SPIs are listed at the beginning of the scenario. We placed the SPIs first to focus attention on those parts of the instructional sequence that will provide opportunities for assessment.

CONTEXT

The context provides some information on the background of the scenario. This background information includes grade level, students' level(s) of English proficiency, language(s) of instruction, instructional focus (e.g., civics class, language arts class, history class), and geographic location within the United States.

BACKGROUND

The background section of each scenario describes in some detail the classroom setting, including the number of ESOL students and mainstream students in the class. This section also identifies the specific focus of the instruction that will be assessed.

ALLOCATION OF TIME

This part explains the time frame in which the instructional and assessment sequence occurs. The amount of time varies across scenarios because each scenario focuses on a different instructional topic and the assessments used in each scenario are tailored to the needs of the students, teachers, and instructional requirements of the lesson(s).

INSTRUCTIONAL AND ASSESSMENT CYCLE

This part of the scenario outlines the instructional and assessment activities implemented in the classroom. Again, our intention is to highlight assessment practices. The activities are organized according to the four phases of the assessment process.

Phase 1: Planning Assessments

In the planning phase, we show how the teacher plans the inclusion of assessment within the instructional unit. In the planning phase, we have included various aspects of assessment for which planning should occur, such as aligning instruction with appropriate assessment; selecting or modifying assessments; and including students, parents, and others in the assessment process. The planning phase is heavily emphasized because, without adequate planning, assessment will not be aligned with instruction and may not account for all the needs of the students. In addition, appropriate assessment requires a great deal of work to ensure that, when the assessment is conducted, it is conducted correctly. Careful planning will help teachers as they incorporate assessment into instruction.

Phase 2: Collecting and Recording Information

In this phase, different types of assessment information are collected through various means. For example, student work pieces may be added to a portfolio; a classroom test may be administered; a teacher may conduct an observation; students may complete a checklist to assess their peers or themselves; or students may write compositions, which the teachers collect. It is important to remember that, in this phase, the assessment information is only collected and recorded.

Phase 3: Analyzing and Interpreting Information

In this phase, the assessment is scored and analyzed. For example, a portfolio may be examined and rated against a set of criteria, a teacher may reflect on a set of checklists students have completed on each of their peers, or students may think about or rate their own performance using a self-assessment. This is the phase in which a teacher would grade classroom tests and look for patterns within the scores of individual students as well as for the entire class.

Phase 4: Reporting and Decision Making

The final phase of the assessment process requires the results of the assessment to be reported to the student, teacher, and all others identified as stakeholders during the assessment process. The results should be reported to stakeholders in meaningful ways. In other words, a graph or chart may not mean anything to first graders, and a large amount of information printed in English may not be understood by all parents. In this phase, it is very important that the results are clear, coherent, and appropriate for the audience. Results may also be used to make decisions about issues ranging from instruction to student placement in ESOL classes. For example, a teacher may realize that one approach to assessment may not yield meaningful information or that it is time to modify instruction.

Throughout the assessment cycle, we have included sample forms to illustrate how assessment can be implemented. Note that we use italics in these sample forms to denote examples of how the form may be used.

DISCUSSION AND REFLECTION

After the four assessment phases, a short discussion follows. The discussion points out important features of the scenario and how these features contribute to meaningful assessments. We also reflect on some ways that the assessment process could be approached differently.

FIGURE 2.1 HOW TO READ THE ESL STANDARDS-BASED ASSESSMENTS

The phrase before the colon is the goal and indicates the focus on social or academic language or sociocultural use of language.

Goal 1, Standard 1, Grades 4–8

The phrase after the colon is the standard and explains what students should be able to do.

To use English to communicate in social settings: Students will use English to participate in social interactions

Sample Progress Indicators

Progress indicators are assessable, observable activities for students to perform to show progress in meeting the standard.

- ask peers for their opinions, preferences, and desires
- elicit information and ask clarification questions
- negotiate solutions to problems, interpersonal misunderstandings, and disputes

Context

Grade Level:	Fourth-grade, self-contained, content-based ESL
English Proficiency Level(s):	Beginning
Language(s) of Instruction:	English
Focus of Instruction:	Social studies
Location:	Urban school district in the Southeast

This section explains the grade and student proficiency levels, instructional focus, and location of the school.

Background

The following scenario describes a fourth-grade, self-contained ESL class in an urban school district serving students from heterogeneous backgrounds. Most students are literate in their first language, and those who are not have been paired with students at higher levels of literacy. This scenario takes place in the first month of the school year. Mr. Thompson, a licensed ESL teacher, teaches the beginning-level immigrant students. Mr. Thompson has observed that his students have limited knowledge of their community. He plans to integrate teaching English with an increased awareness of the neighborhood's resources so that students can feel more at home in their neighborhood.

The background section sets the stage for the classroom scene, describing the teacher and students.

Allocation of Time

This scenario takes place over a 1-week period during four or five 55-minute social studies periods. The first lesson is an introduction to the neighborhood with a role-play activity. The second lesson focuses on student attention during a brainstorming session of community businesses and then proceeds with a walk around the community. The third lesson creates an opportunity for the groups to prepare a pictograph of the information they collected during their walk. In addition, they discuss the importance of local business while they write key phrases. During the fourth lesson, each group presents its pictograph to the class.

28

This section explains the time frame for the instructional and assessment sequence developed in the scenario.

> The instructional and assessment cycle describes the activities in a lesson that shows the standards in action, organized by grade-level clusters.

Instructional and Assessment Cycle

PHASE 1: PLANNING

Mr. Thompson plans a sequence of instructional activities to increase students' knowledge of their community and neighborhood resources. He decides that students will do the following:

1. Draw a map of the neighborhood on chart paper.
2. Talk about the location of the school using prepositions of place.
3. Practice a dialogue between a lost person asking for directions and a police officer who provides directions.
4. Role-play the dialogue.
5. Brainstorm the names of community businesses and resources.
6. Collect informat[ion] neighborhood.
7. Discuss their wa[lk]
8. Create a pictogr[am]
9. Discuss the impo[rtance]
10. Write key words
11. In groups, orally

> The discussion and reflection section provides a brief explanation of student and teacher actions, linking the vignette to the standard and progress indicators.

Discussion and Reflection

This scenario illustrates the continuous assessment process that Mr. Thompson has implemented in his self-contained ESL classroom. It shows how he

- uses one assessment instrument to monitor multiple SPIs
- uses one assessment instrument with similar content taught at different times during

[...]ng and links it to an academic learning context

[...]ning process as well as the product

[...]e of information gained from assessment to use in the [...] future instruction is relevant to the instructional needs of the students.

This scenario has the teacher tallying students' use of prepositional phrases while students practice giving and asking for directions. Performance assessments may not always be the most appropriate approach for measuring discrete-point information. Language is so complex that it may be difficult to home in on one specific skill to the exclusion of others. The assessment task primarily provides targeted information about prepositions to the teacher. This information will be useful in comparing against student progress later in the year.

Connections

- You may notice that Mr. Thompson included plans for integrating the school and larger community into this lesson and assessment plan. At this point in the school year, it would be difficult to assess student progress in understanding such areas. However, as the year progresses, Mr. Thompson will return to this theme and assess student progress since this point in time.

> This section suggests extensions of the scenarios to additional contexts.

[...] show the self-assessment tool and teacher tally sheet to parents [...]ol night, which will occur about 2 weeks after this lesson. An [...] can be used again later in the year to show growth to parents. [...]n similar linguistic backgrounds as Mr. Thompson's students but with higher levels of English proficiency will provide translations for parents as necessary.

- The program has established a database for background information about students. As students enter the school, the following information is entered into this database:
  - amount of schooling in the United States and home country, if any
  - first language
  - oral and written proficiency in first language (L1) and English

	M[...]
	a.
Student	b.
	c.
Student and teacher	M[...] sk[...]
Teacher	A[...] ba[...]

33

CONNECTIONS

In the final part of the scenario, we offer some connections among ESL standards, curriculum, instruction, and assessment and suggest some ways that these connections—between classroom and department, department and district, or among teachers serving ESOL students—can be fostered.

Scenario Topics and Scenario Outline

Figure 2.2 lists the assessment topics addressed in the scenarios, the relevant scenarios, and the appropriate grade levels for the specified scenarios. Following this chart is an outline of a sample scenario (Figure 2.3). We have included this outline to help you in your planning as you weave assessment into your instructional plan.

FIGURE 2.2 TOPICS ADDRESSED IN THE SCENARIOS

Topic	Relevant scenario(s)	Grade level	Page number
District assessment	Goal 1, Standard 2	2	35
	Goal 2, Standard 2	1	54
	Goal 2, Standard 2	11	69
Sharing information across levels	Goal 2, Standard 2	4–5	62
Student profile with background information	Goal 1, Standard 1	4	28
Time lines	Goal 1, Standard 2	2	35
Communication with parents	Goal 1, Standard 1	4	28
	Goal 1, Standard 2	2	35
	Goal 2, Standard 2	1	54
Self-assessment	Goal 1, Standard 1	4	28
	Goal 2, Standard 3	9–11	84
Peer assessment	Goal 1, Standard 3	7	42
	Goal 2, Standard 2	11	69
	Goal 3, Standard 2	10	100
	Goal 3, Standard 3	8	106
Parent assessment	Goal 2, Standard 2	1	54
Collaboration among teachers	Goal 1, Standard 2	2	35
	Goal 2, Standard 1	8	47
	Goal 2, Standard 2	1	54
	Goal 2, Standard 2	11	69
	Goal 2, Standard 3	9–11	84
	Goal 3, Standard 1	all	91
Languages of communication	Goal 2, Standard 1	8	47
	Goal 2, Standard 2	1	54
	Goal 2, Standard 2	4–5	62
	Goal 2, Standard 3	9–11	84
Cultural appropriateness	Goal 2, Standard 2	1	54
	Goal 2, Standard 2	11	69
	Goal 3, Standard 2	10	100
	Goal 3, Standard 3	8	106
Group work	Goal 1, Standard 1	4	28
	Goal 2, Standard 1	8	47
	Goal 2, Standard 2	11	69
	Goal 3, Standard 2	10	100
Standardized tests	Goal 2, Standard 1	8	47
	Goal 2, Standard 2	1	54
	Goal 2, Standard 2	11	69
	Goal 3, Standard 1	all	91
Special needs students	Goal 2, Standard 2	4–5	62

FIGURE 2.3 ASSESSMENT SCENARIO OUTLINE

Goal: _____

Standard: _____

Sample Progress Indicators

-
-
-
-

Context

Grade Level:

English Proficiency Level(s):

Language(s) of Instruction:

Focus of Instruction:

Location:

Background

Allocation of Time

FIGURE 2.3 ASSESSMENT SCENARIO OUTLINE (CONTINUED)

Instructional and Assessment Cycle

Phase 1: Planning

Phase 2: Collecting and Recording Information

Phase 3: Analyzing and Interpreting Information

Phase 4: Reporting and Decision Making

Discussion and Reflection

Connections

Note. This outline may be photocopied for personal use only.

Goal 1, Standard 1, Grades 4–8

To use English to communicate in social settings: Students will use English to participate in social interactions

Sample Progress Indicators

- ask peers for their opinions, preferences, and desires
- elicit information and ask clarification questions
- negotiate solutions to problems, interpersonal misunderstandings, and disputes

Context

Grade Level: Fourth-grade, self-contained, content-based ESL
English Proficiency Level(s):   Beginning
Language(s) of Instruction: English
Focus of Instruction: Social studies
Location: Urban school district in the Southeast

Background

The following scenario describes a fourth-grade, self-contained ESL class in an urban school district serving students from heterogeneous backgrounds. Most students are literate in their first language, and those who are not have been paired with students at higher levels of literacy. This scenario takes place in the first month of the school year. Mr. Thompson, a licensed ESL teacher, teaches the beginning-level immigrant students. Mr. Thompson has observed that his students have limited knowledge of their community. He plans to integrate teaching English with an increased awareness of the neighborhood's resources so that students can feel more at home in their neighborhood.

Allocation of Time

This scenario takes place over a 1-week period during four or five 55-minute social studies periods. The first lesson is an introduction to the neighborhood with a role-play activity. The second lesson focuses on student attention during a brainstorming session of community businesses and then proceeds with a walk around the community. The third lesson creates an opportunity for the groups to prepare a pictograph of the information they collected during their walk. In addition, they discuss the importance of local business while they write key phrases. During the fourth lesson, each group presents its pictograph to the class.

Instructional and Assessment Cycle

PHASE 1: PLANNING

Mr. Thompson plans a sequence of instructional activities to increase students' knowledge of their community and neighborhood resources. He decides that students will do the following:

1. Draw a map of the neighborhood on chart paper.

2. Talk about the location of the school using prepositions of place.

3. Practice a dialogue between a lost person asking for directions and a police officer who provides directions.

4. Role-play the dialogue.

5. Brainstorm the names of community businesses and resources.

6. Collect information on a tally sheet about how students walk to school through the neighborhood.

7. Discuss their walking route with other students.

8. Create a pictograph of the neighborhood using the tally sheet.

9. Discuss the importance of various businesses in the area.

10. Write key words and phrases on the pictograph poster.

11. In groups, orally present the poster that they prepared.

Figure 2.4 shows the various purposes for assessment in this instructional unit.

After reviewing the instructional goals and activities, Mr. Thompson reflects on how he can monitor the students' progress during this activity and incorporate that assessment into

FIGURE 2.4 PURPOSES FOR ASSESSMENT

Student	Monitor progress toward achieving sample progress indicators: a. Ask and express opinions. Assess as students ask peers for their opinions on the importance of various businesses in the area. b. Organize graphically the information collected on the walk. Assess as students work with a group to create the poster, graphically organize the information collected, and orally present it to the class. c. Ask and understand directions using prepositions of place. Assess as students elicit information and ask clarification questions during the dialogue and role-play.
Student and teacher	Measure student awareness of neighborhood resources and introductory map skills.
Teacher	Assess knowledge demonstrated in an academic setting linked to experientially based learning activities.

his overall student assessment. What follows is his plan for integrating assessment into instruction; it describes how each SPI (a, b, c) will be monitored. As part of the planning process, Mr. Thompson carefully selects assessment tools so that he can collect appropriate information.

a+b+c

All three SPIs require peer or group interactions; therefore, in most sections of the lesson, the activities are group based. Mr. Thompson wants to know how well students can work in groups. Although he can observe student interaction patterns during the lesson, he wants to find out from the students themselves how well they think they worked in groups. In addition, he wants to increase student awareness of the importance of working in groups cooperatively. As a result, he selects an instrument designed for self-assessment of group participation.

a+c

During the role-play, when students are asking for and giving directions, the teacher uses a simple tally sheet with the list of target phrases, prepositions of place, and question types listed across the top. Student names are listed down the side. This simple tally sheet can be in the teacher's journal or grade book. This assessment tool will provide Mr. Thompson with information on which language structures have been learned and which need additional practice or reteaching.

a+b+c

Mr. Thompson will collect anecdotal records in his teacher's journal of interactions during the walk and students' presentations of their posters. This will enable him to enhance the learning by reminding students of what they saw and did.

PHASE 2: COLLECTING AND RECORDING INFORMATION
a+b+c

Following the presentation by each group, Mr. Thompson gives the students a self-assessment form to rate their participation in groups and reviews the directions to make sure students know what to do in their groups. (See Figure 2.5.)

a+c

A simple tally sheet (Figure 2.6) can be included in the teacher's journal or grade book. As Mr. Thompson moves between groups listening to the dialogues, he writes the date in the box, indicating that the target phrase or phrases were produced correctly, and he checks off those that were attempted by the student but not yet mastered. During another lesson, later in the term, Mr. Thompson can return to this tally sheet to mark it when the content of another lesson is similar. This way he will know when mastery has occurred.

FIGURE 2.5 SELF-ASSESSMENT FOR GROUP PARTICIPATION

Name:_____ Date:_____

Put a check in the box to show what you did in your group.

In my group	Never	Sometimes	Often
I asked for opinions.			
I gave my opinion.			
I asked for directions.			
I gave directions.			
I asked questions.			
I helped to find answers.			
I agreed or disagreed.			

PHASE 3: ANALYZING AND INTERPRETING INFORMATION

a+b+c

Mr. Thompson analyzes the self-assessment form by summarizing the information from the class on a blank form. The next day, he will report the results to the class. He will highlight the strengths of the class as indicated on the class composite form and select one area that needs improvement for class discussion. Mr. Thompson will keep these forms for reference so that he can compare these results with any similar forms that are used later in the term. This way he can gauge improvement over time.

a+c

The tally sheet serves to chart the use of target phrases students have practiced in their groups and is primarily for teacher information. Appropriate use of these phrases marks progress in reaching SPIs a+c, which are focused on asking questions and negotiating with peers. A summary of the class results can be tallied at the bottom of the sheet (Figure 2.7).

FIGURE 2.6 PREPOSITION TALLY SHEET

Student's name	*on the*	*across from*	*next to*	*where is*	*is it . . . ? (clarification)*
1. Juan					
2. Xiao Yu					
3. Helga					
4. Angel					

FIGURE 2.7 CONTINUATION OF PREPOSITION TALLY SHEET

22. Nina					
23. Miguel					
24. Nora					
25. Oscar					
Number of students who produced phrase and % (number who produced/total number of class)	10 40%	12 48%	6 24%	15 60%	18 72%
Number of students who mastered phrase and % (number who mastered/total number of class)	5 20%	8 32%	3 12%	10 40%	9 36%

By looking at how many students in the class have produced and mastered target phrases, Mr. Thompson can see which target phrases were produced and mastered by whom and which ones may need additional practice in another lesson. He can use the same tally sheet during a future lesson to note improvement.

In analyzing the information on the tally sheet, Mr. Thompson notices that these beginning-level students are starting to ask clarification questions with the phrase *Is it...?* but generally are not yet using the phrase *next to.* Mr. Thompson decides it is necessary to continue practicing all these phrases and to apply them to other map-related activities.

PHASE 4: REPORTING AND DECISION MAKING

Mr. Thompson collects the assessment information as part of his continuous assessment process. During the week following the lesson, he shares the results of the self-assessment with the class. Because this is the first time he has used such an assessment with his class, he will spend more time discussing the results with individual students than he will in the future. Mr. Thompson sets up conferences with five or six students a day for 5 minutes each to discuss the results of the student's self assessment and his tally sheet on the student's use of target phrases. Using this information, Mr. Thompson and the student will set some individual student goals for participation in groups during the first quarter.

Later in the semester, Mr. Thompson will use this and other information to discuss with and prepare reports for parents. During this conference time with parents, he will also review progress toward achieving the student's goal for group participation.

Discussion and Reflection

This scenario illustrates the continuous assessment process that Mr. Thompson has implemented in his self-contained ESL classroom. It shows how he

- uses one assessment instrument to monitor multiple SPIs

- uses one assessment instrument with similar content taught at different times during the school term

- documents experiential learning and links it to an academic learning context

- focuses assessment on the learning process as well as the product

Mr. Thompson analyzes each piece of information gained from assessment to use in the decision-making process and to ensure future instruction is relevant to the instructional needs of the students.

This scenario has the teacher tallying students' use of prepositional phrases while students practice giving and asking for directions. Performance assessments may not always be the most appropriate approach for measuring discrete-point information. Language is so complex that it may be difficult to home in on one specific skill to the exclusion of others. The assessment task primarily provides targeted information about prepositions to the teacher. This information will be useful in comparing against student progress later in the year.

Connections

- You may notice that Mr. Thompson included plans for integrating the school and larger community into this lesson and assessment plan. At this point in the school year, it would be difficult to assess student progress in understanding such areas. However, as the year progresses, Mr. Thompson will return to this theme and assess student progress since this point in time.

- Mr. Thompson will show the self-assessment tool and teacher tally sheet to parents during Back-to-School night, which will occur about 2 weeks after this lesson. An updated tally sheet can be used again later in the year to show growth to parents. Older students from similar linguistic backgrounds as Mr. Thompson's students but with higher levels of English proficiency will provide translations for parents as necessary.

- The program has established a database for background information about students. As students enter the school, the following information is entered into this database:
  — amount of schooling in the United States and home country, if any
  — first language
  — oral and written proficiency in first language (L1) and English

— country of origin

— date of entry into the program

Figure 2.8 provides an example of a student information form for collecting this kind of data.

When students leave Mr. Thompson's class, the district will continue to gather data on student achievement and will analyze these data using the above variables. This will provide important information about students' successes or additional needs for support. It will also assist administrators in making data-driven decisions about program services.

FIGURE 2.8 STUDENT INFORMATION SHEET

Student name: _____

              Surname   First given name   Second name

Student identification number: _____

Date of birth: _____ Current grade level: _____

Home language: _____

Current language proficiency classification: _____

Present schooling:

- Type of program of instruction _____

- Medium of instruction (English/native language) _____

Previous schooling:

In the United States

- Number of years _____

- Type of program of instruction _____

- Medium of instruction (English/native language) _____

Outside the United States

- Number of years _____

- Type of program of instruction _____

- Medium of instruction (English/native language) _____

Goal 1, Standard 2, Grades Pre-K–3

To use English to communicate in social settings: Students will interact in, through, and with spoken and written English for personal expression and enjoyment

Sample Progress Indicators

- describe favorite storybook characters
- recommend a book to a peer
- ask information questions for personal reasons
- make requests for personal reasons

Context

Grade Level: Second-grade transitional bilingual class
English Proficiency Level(s):   Intermediate
Language(s) of Instruction: English and Spanish (however, these library assessments are primarily for English)
Focus of Instruction: Reading (and oral communication)
Location: Urban school district in the Southeast

Background

This scenario describes events in a second-grade transitional bilingual class in an urban school district. All students are native Spanish speakers, learning English and Spanish in school. The teacher, Ms. Huartado, a native Spanish speaker herself, learned English after moving to the United States from Mexico as a teenager. Some of her students are from Mexico and Central and South America, but many were born in the United States to families from Central America. Most first heard English when entering kindergarten and thus have about $2\frac{1}{2}$ years of English language development.

Allocation of Time

This is an ongoing unit that continues throughout the school year. Ms. Huartado takes the students to the library once a week for a 50-minute period.

Instructional and Assessment Cycle

PHASE 1: PLANNING

Ms. Huartado uses the English language objectives from her district to guide oral language assessment and planning. She also has a list of technology objectives for all second graders in the state. In addition, her school plan includes goals for boosting parent-school communication. She plans to weave these together as part of her library visit objectives and assessment. She intends to help students

- talk to peers about their favorite books and characters

- ask questions of peers and adults about books and library procedures

- interact with parents and other adults who visit the class to share favorite books

- use the Internet to send e-mail messages about books and become aware of resources available for information gathering

- present information to the whole class about a favorite book

Ms. Huartado plans to use weekly library visits to monitor student progress over time with these objectives. She divides the class into four heterogeneous groups (A, B, C, and D) so that students have an opportunity to talk about books in small groups. Generally, during their weekly library visits, students will look for books to check out and occasionally listen to a story read by the librarian. Ms. Huartado also plans to invite parents to read storybooks in Spanish or English and to have students log on to the computers in the library to introduce Internet and e-mail skills. Although students will continue to share their books informally, she also wants to structure a book talk in which each student shares his or her book with the whole group on a monthly basis.

Her monthly plan for the 50-minute library visits is as follows (with each activity designed to take roughly 15 minutes):

Week 1:

1. Check out book(s)
2. Listen to story by Mr. Gosler (the librarian)
3. Group A book talk (four students)

Week 2:

1. Check out book(s)
2. Engage in one computer-related minilesson
3. Group B book talk (five students)

Week 3:

1. Check out book(s)
2. Listen to a parent share a favorite book

3. Group C book talk (four students)

4. Send e-mail to pen pals

Week 4:

1. Check out book(s)

2. Group D book talk (five students)

3. Open time (e.g., reading with a buddy)

4. Send e-mail to pen pals

To keep track of the data to be collected, Ms. Huartado sets up a weekly and monthly schedule (Figure 2.9). Note that Ms. Huartado collects some data on some students during every library visit.

PHASE 2: COLLECTING AND RECORDING INFORMATION

To monitor students' progress in working toward the targeted SPIs, Ms. Huartado collects data from four different sources throughout the year.

Anecdotal Records

At the weekly library visits, she writes anecdotal records on a clipboard. Monthly, she reviews her notes and transfers the information to more formal checklists as described later in the scenario. Ms. Huartado records information on an anecdotal form with boxes for each

FIGURE 2.9 PLAN FOR COLLECTING DATA

September	October	November	December
Week 1 • Anecdotal records–Group C • Book talk records–Group A	Week 1	Week 1	Week 1
Week 2 • Anecdotal records–Group D • Book talk records–Group B	Week 2	Week 2	Week 2
Week 3 • Anecdotal records–Group A • Book talk records–Group C	Week 3	Week 3	Week 3
Week 4 • Anecdotal records–Group B • Book talk records–Group D	Week 4	Week 4	Week 4
Teacher Reminders: *Keep track of all books the students check out; check progress by end of November.* *Keep track of e-mail proficiency; use district-level checklist.* *Make notes on parent visits (sporadically noted).*			

student and a place to record the skill being observed at the top. Her shorthand for recording notes is as follows:

- If someone asks a peer a comprehensible question about a book, she writes Q-P. If the student asks her or another adult, she writes Q-A.

- If someone shares information informally about a book he or she has read, she writes SH-P or SH-A (for peer or adult).

- After she has modeled the "five finger rule" for determining if a book is too hard, she records who successfully and independently uses this rule by writing a 5 next to the name. This rule suggests that a student who is unfamiliar with more than five words on a page is reading a book that is too hard and should choose a book at a lower reading level.

- When time permits, she also makes note of changes in vocabulary, phrases, and verb tenses she hears because they are all part of the oral language rubric from the district.

Classroom Checklist

When Ms. Huartado modeled the book talk in September, her class helped her generate criteria for an excellent talk. As students present their book talk to the class, she fills out a checklist based on the student-generated criteria (Figure 2.10).

District-Level Checklist

Students take turns practicing their e-mail skills on the library's computers. The long-term goal is to write an e-mail to a reading buddy in a neighboring school. As they successfully complete this, she checks off this goal on a checklist of district-level objectives for second-grade technology skills.

FIGURE 2.10 BOOK TALK CHECKLIST

Name: _____ Date: _____

Book read: _____

The student:

_____ told the title.

_____ told the author's name.

_____ told the illustrator (if any).

_____ told who the favorite character was and one reason why.

_____ briefly described the _____ beginning _____ middle _____ end.

_____ gave two reasons why he or she liked or disliked the book.

_____ shared two favorite pictures.

_____ spoke clearly and with enthusiasm.

Parent Notes

When parents visit the library with her students, she makes note of what students ask and tell them in her anecdotal records.

PHASE 3: ANALYZING AND INTERPRETING INFORMATION

Because these library visits take place throughout the year, the process of assessment is fluid and influences instruction.

At the end of each month and grading period, Ms. Huartado checks her anecdotal records. She marks progress for each individual student by highlighting new skills on the district rubric. Each marking period she changes the color of her highlighter.

As Ms. Huartado reviews and records monthly data, she makes note of skills that seem to be needed by all or many students. For instance, she notes that the same three students asked all the questions during book talks or that many students struggled to give reasons when starting a sentence such as *I like this book because. . . .* She designs minilessons to help students with these skills and then designs a way to note progress in her anecdotal records.

Ms. Huartado uses the technology checklist data to plan further minilessons on the computer. She shares information with the students about interesting author and book Web sites and notices that the information influences the books they check out in future weeks. They receive responses from their e-mail pen pals, which also lead to new enthusiasm for books.

The school planning team has given her a form on which to record and classify all parent contact and visits, and, in her monthly reviews, she tabulates and transfers the data. She marks who visited, how long they stayed, what activities they engaged in, and what language they spoke in. She also does some personal reflecting and note-taking on what methods seem to help parents feel welcome in the school.

PHASE 4: REPORTING AND DECISION MAKING

- Ms. Huartado uses the oral rubrics she highlighted to communicate progress to parents and the students' other teachers, and she also uses the data to evaluate students for an oral grade on their report cards.

- Ms. Huartado shares the checklist she filled out during the book talks with each student, answering any questions and offering advice for next time. Then she files the form in her assessment portfolio for each student. She also discusses the results with other teachers, such as the school reading specialist, to keep tabs on students who might need extra assistance or enrichment.

- Ms. Huartado shares the technology checklist data with the school's technology resource teacher so that future computer lab lessons can extend what students already know. Eventually, in fifth grade, students will take a statewide standardized test on technology, so it is important that Ms. Huartado coordinate lessons and share student progress with other teachers at the school.

- The parent data are used by the school committee to assess parent involvement in the schools and plan for future parent interactions. Ms. Huartado also uses the data and her reflections during a faculty meeting on encouraging parent participation in school activities.

Discussion and Reflection

Teachers may find that their work situation does not resemble the one discussed in this scenario. Some potential modifications for this plan follow.

1. For an ESL pullout or inclusion program

   - In a multilingual situation, pay attention to students' native language needs. Encourage parents from many cultures to come and share their books (or songs, stories, or artwork) with the class. Work with the librarian to provide books in many languages.

   - Collaborate with the classroom teacher to plan and assess. Think about mutual goals, such as choosing appropriate books, and also goals specific to your students, such as learning to ask a comprehensible question.

2. For the teacher who needs a streamlined process because of lack of time or very demanding students

   - Carry index cards or self-adhesive notes in your pocket and make anecdotal notes here and there. Some teachers like self-adhesive notes because they can attach them to assessment pages later without recopying data.

   - Use walkabout time to help high-need students, and save the book talk time for your assessments. This is not as genuine a reflection of informal student speech, but it is one option.

   - Eliminate the technology and parent goals and focus on oral goals for all students. Look for growth in many skills for all students, however, because oral language learning does not follow a clear and consistent trajectory. Also, invite parents to participate even if you are not assessing their interactions with students—it is still motivating for young readers.

3. For the teacher who wants to make a stronger connection between the school community and the public library

   - Invite a librarian (preferably a bilingual one) from the nearest local library to address the PTA or come to a school function to meet with parents.

   - Have applications for public library cards available for any parents who come to the school or to your classroom.

   - Enlist librarians to enable parents to check books out of the school library. This is useful for busy parents or those who cannot easily get to the nearest library because of transportation problems.

Connections

- Using parents as L1 reading resources helps students develop and maintain good reading skills in their L1. Strong L1 reading skills foster English language reading skills. By viewing parents' languages as resources, teachers also strengthen parent-school connections because parents are welcomed as active participants in their children's education.

- By using complementary assessments, teachers can more accurately determine progress on district standards. In this scenario, the teacher used a variety of assessment approaches, including some she developed herself as well as a district-based checklist.

Goal 1, Standard 3, Grades 4–8

To use English to communicate in social settings: Students will use learning strategies to extend their communicative competence

Sample Progress Indicators

- use a dictionary to validate choice of language
- ask a classmate whether a particular word or phrase is correct
- keep individual notes for language learning
- test appropriate use of new vocabulary, phrases, and structures

Context

Grade Level:	Seventh-grade science class
English Proficiency Level(s):	Beginning–advanced
Language(s) of Instruction:	English
Focus of Instruction:	Science
Location:	Urban school district in the Northwest

Background

The scenario takes place in a heterogeneous seventh-grade science class for both ESOL and non-ESOL students. ESOL students range in proficiency from beginning to advanced. The teacher is Spanish/English bilingual. This scenario shows how students use conferencing, self-checklists, and peer assessments to assess their use of learning strategies during a class field trip to the science museum. It demonstrates how these assessments allow students to constantly monitor their use of learning strategies to extend their communicative competence.

Allocation of Time

In this scenario, students reflect on how they use learning strategies during a class field trip. This instructional sequence takes about 1 week.

Instructional and Assessment Cycle

PHASE 1: PLANNING

Mr. Amado prepares students for the field trip to the science museum by reviewing some of their learning strategies and approaches to assessing their use of learning strategies. He decides that he will

- review the classroom checklist for learning strategies with students

- encourage discussion before and after the field trip to highlight the use of strategies during the field trip

- discuss the learning strategies via journals and conferencing

After reviewing his instructional goals and activities, Mr. Amado will reflect on how he can monitor students' progress in using learning strategies throughout the school year and on this field trip (see Figure 2.11). Because SPIs are generic indicators designed to be used across content areas, Mr. Amado must develop specific assessment activities that reflect the content of his class. He has already established checklists for student journals and peer assessment processes for ongoing assessment.

Next, Mr. Amado reviews the checklists that he and the students have developed to keep track of the different learning strategies. He decides to focus on a few learning strategies (using a dictionary, asking a classmate for assistance, keeping notes in a journal, and testing different uses of new vocabulary) for this lesson.

PHASE 2: COLLECTING AND RECORDING INFORMATION

Mr. Amado reviews the checklist procedures as well as peer assessment, journals, and conferencing procedures with the students. For this assignment, the checklist is a way to recall how different strategies are used (see Figure 2.13).

- Using the checklist, students report in their journals some of the learning strategies they used during the field trip. Later that month, students will use the journals as a basis for discussion in their conferences with Mr. Amado.

FIGURE 2.11 PURPOSES FOR ASSESSMENT

Stakeholders	Purposes for assessment
Student	Monitor progress toward achieving sample progress indicators: • use a dictionary to validate choice of language • ask a classmate whether a particular word or phrase is correct • keep individual notes for language learning • test appropriate use of new vocabulary, phrases, and structures
Teacher	Determine the effectiveness of different learning strategies in helping students of different proficiency levels participate in a field trip.
Peers	Help each other apply learning strategies.

FIGURE 2.12 ALIGNING PURPOSE AND ASSESSMENT

Purposes	Collection tools	Recording tools
Monitor use of dictionaries	Peer discussion, conferencing	Checklist, journal
Monitor student progress in checking with peers on word usage	Peer discussion	Checklist, journal
Monitor student performance in learning several strategies	Journal	Checklist, journal

- Mr. Amado uses student journals to chart their progress in using different learning strategies.

- Students meet with one another to review the learning strategies they employed during the field trip.

In this assessment phase, Mr. Amado selected specific tools for collecting and recording information (see Figure 2.12). Samples of some of the tools exemplified some approaches to collecting and recording the information.

Learning Strategies Checklist

The students use the checklist in Figure 2.13 before and after their field trip, first to recall some learning strategies and then to assess the use of those strategies. Developing this checklist took a good portion of a class period, but Mr. Amado felt the time was well spent because the process elicited input from students and focused their attention on learning strategies. They provided suggestions on different categories for assessment.

Peer Discussion

Using the checklist, students talk to one another about different strategies they used on the field trip. They also discuss which strategies worked well and which ones did not. Then they talk about why one strategy worked better than another.

FIGURE 2.13 LEARNING STRATEGIES CHECKLIST

Student name:	Date:
	Yes/No (circle)
Uses dictionary to look up words.	Y N
Asks other students for help with words.	Y N
Asks teacher for help with vocabulary.	Y N
Practices using new vocabulary.	Y N
Asks other students if new vocabulary is used correctly.	Y N
Asks teacher if new vocabulary is used correctly.	Y N

Student Journals

After discussing the checklists with other students, students take some time to write in their journals about the strategies they used. They examine earlier journal entries and write about the progress they have made in using learning strategies. They also discuss which learning strategies worked best for them and what they can do to use more learning strategies.

Conferencing

Based on this and other journal entries, students have information for their quarterly conference or check-in with the teacher. The check-in takes only a few minutes, but it allows Mr. Amado a little time to review the student's class work and progress in using learning strategies. Conferences take place in English, Spanish, or both.

PHASE 3: ANALYZING AND INTERPRETING INFORMATION

As he collects information about students' performance on each of the activities in this unit, Mr. Amado analyzes the information so that he can adjust his instruction and provide feedback to students.

- To check on students' use of strategies, Mr. Amado reads the journals. He uses the journals to find out which strategies are working for students.

- While students discuss the strategies used during the field trip, Mr. Amado walks around and listens. He hears students discussing frankly how the strategies help them and how they may be confusing.

- Mr. Amado uses his quarterly conferences to help students work toward using effective learning strategies. He also finds out which strategies are working for the whole class and which ones might need clarification.

PHASE 4: REPORTING AND DECISION MAKING

Mr. Amado uses the information he collected in several ways:

- He uses his review of student journals to examine his classroom practice. For example, if many students are having trouble using the Spanish/English dictionaries, he might review the dictionary with the whole class. He might also find out that there are not enough dictionaries for all students and may talk to the administration about finding more dictionaries.

- From listening to the peer discussions of strategy use, Mr. Amado learns about students' frustrations and successes because they are honest with one another. He uses this information to review the use of strategies with his class.

- During these discussions, Mr. Amado also learns which strategies are most and least helpful to individual students. For example, a shy student may prefer to use a dictionary rather than ask another student for clarification. A more advanced student may need to ask another advanced student or non-ESOL student for help, whereas a beginning student may be best at asking another speaker of the same language.

- Mr. Amado uses this information to report on the use of learning strategies with his colleagues.

Discussion and Reflection

This scenario illustrates how assessment activities can be interwoven within an instructional sequence. It shows how Mr. Amado

- encourages students to use learning strategies outside the classroom during a field trip

- allows students to rely on one another, both for employing learning strategies and for reflecting on how strategies can help them

- uses the information to help students and other teachers in the school to continue using learning strategies

Ongoing assessment is interwoven into the fabric of the classroom. Information gained from everyday interaction from students, such as participation in class discussion, is internal to the functioning of that classroom. Students and the teacher receive feedback that reinforces student behaviors and informs instruction.

For example, based on the information collected during assessment, Mr. Amado realizes that several of the targeted SPIs are more readily assessed if students are paired prior to the museum field trip. The peer discussion and Learning Strategies Checklist, for example, would have yielded better results if the teacher had assigned partners based on the students' language proficiency and language backgrounds.

Connections

Learning strategies are an important part of helping students become conscious of their language development. Mr. Amado has found a way to include using learning strategies in the more relaxed atmosphere of a field trip. This application helps emphasize that learning strategies are important for everyday life and communication.

Goal 3, Standard 3, shows another approach to assessing learning strategies. Refer to this scenario to find another perspective on learning strategy assessment.

Goal 2, Standard 1, Grades 4–8

To use English to achieve academically in all content areas: Students will use English to interact in the classroom

Goal 2, Standard 2

To use English to achieve academically in all content areas: Students will use English to obtain, process, construct, and provide subject matter information in spoken and written form

Goal 2, Standard 3

To use English to achieve academically in all content areas: Students will use appropriate learning strategies to construct and apply academic knowledge

In this scenario, we have tried to reflect the common classroom practice that teachers interweave multiple educational objectives into one instructional sequence. In this case, Ms. Smith-Sung is targeting SPIs across three ESL standards.

Sample Progress Indicators

GOAL 2, STANDARD 1

- share classroom materials and work successfully with a partner
- paraphrase a teacher's directions orally

- modify a statement made by a peer

- ask for assistance with a task

- request supplies to complete an assignment

GOAL 2, STANDARD 2

- gather and organize the appropriate materials needed to complete a task

- synthesize, analyze, and evaluate information

- define, compare, and classify objects

- record observations

GOAL 2, STANDARD 3

- make pictures to check comprehension of a story or process

- rephrase, explain, revise, and expand oral or written information to check comprehension

- seek more knowledgeable others with whom to consult to advance understanding

- seek out print and nonprint resources in the native language when needed

Context

Grade Level:	Eighth-grade sheltered science class
English Proficiency Level(s):	Variety of levels; high beginning–advanced
Language(s) of Instruction:	English (with 5-minute overviews of activities in Vietnamese and Spanish)
Focus of Instruction:	Science
Location:	Urban school district in the West

Background

The following scenario unfolds in a self-contained, eighth-grade science classroom in an urban school district. The class consists mostly of immigrant students from Vietnam, Central America, and Mexico. All the students are high beginning- to advanced-level ESL students. The teacher has training and experience working with ESOL students. Two bilingual instructional assistants work in the class on a daily basis. One is a Spanish/English speaker; the other is a Vietnamese/English speaker.

Allocation of Time

The key concepts of this unit of study associated with the scientific method are introduced early in the year and then systematically incorporated into subsequent units. Initially, a 45-minute period each day for 1 week is devoted to familiarizing the students with the multiple SPIs associated with Goal 2, Standards 1, 2, and 3. Students in this sheltered content class are expected to apply the information and strategies learned to the standardized state test that is administered midyear of eighth grade.

Instructional and Assessment Cycle

PHASE 1: PLANNING

Ms. Smith-Sung, the science teacher, integrates the SPIs of Goal 2, Standards 1, 2, and 3, so students will have ample opportunities to interact with one another in acquiring skills and strategies in a content-based classroom. Her academic goal is to have students use metric measurement, in particular that associated with volume, as a basis for learning the scientific method. Her language goals are to have students negotiate with one another and explain a process. Instructional assessment activities are designed for both content and language goals for each of the 5 days of the unit:

Content Goal	*Language Goal*
Day 1: Classify and log observations	Hypothesize and make predictions
Day 2: Paraphrase expository text	Explain scientific method
Day 3: Complete graphic organizer	Negotiate with peers
Day 4: Organize steps of scientific method	Receive feedback from peers
Day 5: Apply test-taking strategies	Review answers to questions

PHASE 2: COLLECTING AND RECORDING INFORMATION

Having developed the academic and language goals for the unit based on the ESL standards and SPIs, Ms. Smith-Sung's next step in the alignment of curriculum, instruction, and assessment is to specify how she will collect and record information from the students. Because it is the beginning of the school year, Ms. Smith-Sung decides to select some instructional assessment methods that will become the mainstay of her class, namely, the use of graphic organizers, a log of the science labs, and a strategies inventory.

Day 1

Each group of students first makes a prediction of the volume of four containers and agrees on their estimated capacity. Several students ask the instructional assistants to clarify the directions for the task in their native language; others rely on their peers with more advanced English language proficiency for help. Students then record the results in their individual science logs (see Figure 2.14). The group with the closest estimate shares the strategies they used for measuring the volume of the container.

Day 2

Ms. Smith-Sung introduces the steps of the scientific method based on the lab exercise the students completed the previous day. She facilitates a discussion that involves the entire class producing a language experience story that she writes on the board. Students then pair up and paraphrase the multistep process to their partner.

FIGURE 2.14 SCIENCE LOG

Container	Estimated capacity (in milliliters)	True capacity	Difference between estimated and true capacities
1.			
2.			
3.			
4.			

Day 3

The students, in their same cooperative groups as Day 1, review the steps of the scientific method. Some refer to the language experience story still on the board from the previous day; others seek native language support by scanning science books available in Spanish and a worksheet in Vietnamese. After reaching consensus on how to interpret each step for the experiment conducted on Day 1, the recorder of each group completes the graphic organizer displayed in Figure 2.15.

Day 4

As a review, Ms. Smith-Sung hands the students an envelope containing a series of seven strip sentences with the steps of the scientific method. First, they put the sentences in chronological order and then are instructed to illustrate or describe each step in writing. Next, Ms. Smith-Sung discusses with the students the learning strategies highlighted from the SPIs for Goal 2, Standard 3. The students list the strategies in their individual inventories and give an example of how each one has been used that week in science class (see Figure 2.16). Next, the students, in pairs, share the examples of the strategies with each other.

Day 5

The students take a multiple-choice test on the scientific method designed by the teacher that incorporates pictures, their graphic organizer used in instruction, and some written expository text. When all have finished, the students exchange papers. Ms. Smith-Sung reviews the questions, the partners grade each other's responses, and individual students explain their choices.

FIGURE 2.15 GRAPHIC ORGANIZER FOR THE SCIENTIFIC METHOD

The scientific method: Steps in the process	For our experiment, we
1. Identify the problem.	1.
2. Make observations.	2.
3. State hypothesis.	3.
4. Test hypothesis.	4.
5. Collect data.	5.
6. Analyze data.	6.
7. Make conclusions.	7.

FIGURE 2.16 LEARNING STRATEGIES INVENTORY

Learning strategy	An example of how I used it
1. Make pictures to check comprehension of a process.	*I drew pictures for the experiment.*
2. Rephrase written information to check comprehension.	*I talked with my friend about the scientific method.*
3. Ask a classmate or adult for help.	
4. Refer to books or worksheets in the native language when needed.	

PHASE 3: ANALYZING AND INTERPRETING INFORMATION

Ms. Smith-Sung analyzes the data on each of the instructional assessment activities with documentation forms that are aligned with the ESL standards. At the beginning of every academic year, Ms. Smith-Sung meets with other ESL teachers in the district and, together, they have an opportunity to design prototypes for data collection, recording, and analysis. This year, the teachers created forms for Goal 2, Standards 1 and 3.

For Goal 2, Standard 1, an ESL teacher volunteers to develop a checklist for ESL and classroom teachers in the district for recording oral interaction of ESOL students. She thinks of creating a broad classification scheme and decides that "Interaction with teachers and adults," and "Interaction with peers" would capture all the SPIs. As students need to demonstrate the use of multiple interaction patterns over time, columns are created for teachers to date each occurrence. Ms. Smith-Sung puts the checklist on a clipboard and, as she teaches and observes the students interact, she notes the occurrence (see Figure 2.17).

For Goal 2, Standard 3, the teachers decide that in all content-based ESL classes (math, social studies, and science), students will maintain a running inventory of academic learning strategies, such as the one illustrated in this scenario. At the end of each quarter, the students tally how many times a specific strategy (or SPI) has been used and discuss this with their teacher during a conference. The teacher, in turn, has a master list of the learning strategies and transfers the information from each student at the time of the conference.

FIGURE 2.17 ORAL INTERACTION CHECKLIST

Interaction with teachers and adults	Date	Date	Date	Date	Date	Date
Paraphrase a teacher's directions orally.						
Request supplies to complete an assignment.						
Interaction with peers						
Share classroom materials and work with a partner.						
Modify a statement made by a peer.						

PHASE 4: REPORTING AND DECISION MAKING

Ms. Smith-Sung, as well as the other junior high school teachers, uses a point system to determine grades. In this scenario, each academic and language goal for the week is assigned points, according to its importance, that are added to produce a final score (see Figure 2.18). Later in the year, Ms. Smith-Sung plans to modify this type of reporting form to use as a weekly planning sheet for the students and as a format for peer and student self-assessment.

Discussion and Reflection

Teachers often simultaneously address multiple standards in their classrooms. Therefore, in this scenario, there is a blending of three ESL standards and SPIs within the instruction and assessment cycle. This integrated approach to standards-based instruction is a realistic portrayal of what occurs in many classrooms.

Given the multiple purposes for assessment, Ms. Smith-Sung uses several different ways of collecting, analyzing, and reporting data. She carefully matches her instruction and assessment with the standards and reporting forms. The figures in this scenario illustrate the alignment among the phases of assessment. Alignment is key to having valid assessment.

In this content-based classroom, Ms. Smith-Sung is careful to balance the measurement of the students' language development and academic achievement; each day she addresses a language and academic goal. However, in her instruction and assessment, the language and academic targets are intertwined. A language-rich, academically challenging learning environment contributes to the success of ESOL students in school.

FIGURE 2.18 SCIENCE GRADE REPORT SHEET

Science Class: The Scientific Method		
Content goal	**Possible points**	**My points**
Show how to		
A.1. classify and log observations.	10	_____
A.2. explain scientific method.	10	_____
A.3. complete graphic organizer.	10	_____
A.4. organize steps of scientific method.	10	_____
A.5. apply test-taking strategies.	25	_____
Language goal		
Use language to		
L.1 hypothesize and make predictions.	10	_____
L.2. paraphrase expository text.	10	_____
L.3. negotiate with peers.	5	_____
L.4. receive feedback from peers.	5	_____
L.5. review answers to questions.	5	_____
Total points for the week	100	Grade: _____

Connections

Standardized testing for ESOL students, especially when high-stake measures carry consequences for students, is one of the most challenging issues that currently faces our field. There is a tension between two camps: those who wish to maximize the equity and validity of the assessment and those who wish to maximize inclusion of ESOL students, irrespective of the measure. Some states have developed alternate assessment systems for students receiving bilingual/ESL support. Others have a stipulated time span when ESOL students are exempt from large-scale, standardized achievement testing. Still others have approved a set of accommodations (e.g., administration in small groups, use of bilingual glossaries, translation of directions) that may be used with ESOL students during district and state testing. Teachers should be aware of the policies that apply to students with whom they work and prepare them accordingly.

ESOL students should not be immune from testing per se, as it is such an integral part of U.S. school culture. Teacher or classroom tests, as part of sound assessment, should be an extension of what occurs during instruction. Note, for example, that the test Ms. Smith-Sung devises includes the graphic organizer with which the students are familiar. This principle applies to large-scale assessment. If students are afforded accommodations in large-scale situations, they should be identical to those experienced in their daily instruction.

Goal 2, Standard 2, Grades Pre-K–3

To use English to achieve academically in all content areas: Students will use English to obtain, process, construct, and provide subject matter information in spoken and written form

Sample Progress Indicators

- identify and associate written symbols with words (e.g., written numerals with spoken numbers, the compass rose with directional words)
- define, compare, and classify objects (e.g., according to number, shape, color, size, function, physical characteristics)
- record observations
- construct a chart or other graphic showing data

Context

Grade Level: First-grade bilingual class
English Proficiency Level(s):   Mostly beginning; a few intermediate
Language(s) of Instruction: Spanish and English
Focus of Instruction: Mathematics
Location: Suburban school district in the East

Background

The following scenario takes places in a Spanish/English bilingual first-grade class in a suburban school district. The class consists mostly of immigrant students from the Dominican Republic and a few students of Puerto Rican descent. The class is taught by a certified English/Spanish bilingual teacher with ESL training. Most of the students have a beginning level of proficiency in English, although a few are at a low intermediate level. The students, however, are at different levels of academic (reading and math) readiness. It is early in the school year.

Allocation of Time

This scenario occurs over a 2-week time span. Instruction and assessment activities are incorporated into the math period of approximately one 30-minute period each day. The culminating project, which extends into the home, is an application of what students have done at school.

WEEK 1

The first week is devoted to the students developing the concept of measurement. Students engage in kinesthetic activities, work with real objects, and practice describing what they are doing. Mr. Quintana, the bilingual teacher, takes anecdotal notes on an observation checklist. At the end of the week, Mr. Quintana models several bar graph displays based on measurement, introduces a task-specific checklist to the students, and sends a checklist home for use with family members.

WEEK 2

The students move from concrete to more abstract measurement activities. During this time, they manipulate unifix cubes in various ways. After the students create their unifix bar graph and match the appropriate numerals, Mr. Quintana explains the project that they are to complete at home. As students bring in their projects, the teacher conducts an individual student conference and completes a summary checklist for Goal 2, Standard 2.

Instructional and Assessment Cycle

PHASE 1: PLANNING

Mr. Quintana plans a project consisting of a sequence of instructional and assessment activities to help support students in understanding basic measurement concepts. He decides that, over the next 2 weeks, the students will

- give instructions to the teacher on how to arrange towers of varying sizes according to height

- practice using measurement vocabulary, such as *smallest* and *tallest*

- participate in a whole-body activity to construct a group (or class) height continuum and describe relative ranking

- work in pairs to arrange objects by height

- complete a worksheet that matches actual unifix cubes to drawings of unifix cubes and then write the numerals below the figures on the worksheet

- make and interpret a bar graph using unifix cubes

- construct a bar graph based on the heights of family members or lengths of their hands

Mr. Quintana first reviews his general instructional goals for the class. Then, he decides on some ways to assess students for the individual activities and the bar graph project he has designed. There are multiple audiences or stakeholders involved in the assessment of this project: students, family members, and teachers. Each group brings a unique perspective and has a distinct purpose for assessment, as shown in Figure 2.19.

The remaining phases of the assessment cycle are presented according to these audiences. In this way, there is built-in continuity from phase to phase that helps ensure validity of the assessment.

PHASE 2: COLLECTING AND RECORDING INFORMATION
Student

Mr. Quintana collects and records information pertaining to the stated SPIs using a variety of approaches. For each student, Mr. Quintana plans to

- use an observation checklist as students work in pairs

- make anecdotal notes on student performance in giving instructions and comparing heights of objects

- check the student math worksheet for accuracy

- use a task-specific rating scale created for the bar graph project (see Figure 2.20)

Family Member(s)

Mr. Quintana sends a letter home in English and Spanish to the families of students in his class explaining the objectives of the project and how family members may assist in instruction and assessment. He asks a family member to complete a checklist of concepts and activities related to the project (see Figure 2.21). On one side, the checklist is in Spanish and, on the other side, it is in English.

PHASE 3: ANALYZING AND INTERPRETING INFORMATION
Student

Mr. Quintana analyzes and interprets the qualitative and quantitative information he has collected and recorded for his class. Again, he relies on multiple forms of assessment to

FIGURE 2.19 PURPOSES FOR ASSESSMENT

Student	Monitor academic achievement and progress toward attaining stated SPIs as applied to mathematics, social studies, and ESL.
Family member(s)	Reflect on specific student skills associated with constructing a bar graph.
District bilingual and mainstream teachers	Determine if students in the bilingual section are keeping pace with other first-grade students in mainstream classes.

FIGURE 2.20 TASK-SPECIFIC RATING SCALE

The Bar Graph Project

Student: *Juan Carlos Moya*   Grade: *1*

School year: *2000*

Languages of instruction and assessment: *Spanish* (L1) *and English* (L2)

Directions: Mark the extent to which the student demonstrates attainment of the stated sample progress indicator on the bar graph project by writing the numeral 1, 2, or 3 in the appropriate content-area box. To the right, note the date and data source used for evidence of the rating.

1 = Not yet evident   2 = Occasionally evident   3 = Consistently evident

Sample progress indicator	Language used	Math	ESL	Social studies	Evidence and date
Arrange objects by height	L1, L2	3			*Observation family checklist 10/5*
Describe objects	L2		1		*Anecdotal notes 10/7*
Compare objects	L2		3		*Anecdotal notes 10/9*
Draw objects and write numeral	L1, L2	2			*Worksheet 10/10*
Construct and interpret unifix bar graph	L1, L2	2			*Observation 10/12*
Construct bar graph of family members	L1			2	*Bar graph display 10/15*

ascertain the extent to which his students are progressing toward the attainment of Goal 2, Standard 2. Specifically, for each student, Mr. Quintana will

- respond by following the student's oral directions and probe student's language use

- complete District Summary Checklist for Goal 2, Standard 2 (see Figure 2.22)

- have a conference during which the student discusses and explains his or her bar graph

District Bilingual and Mainstream Teachers

Mr. Quintana participates in professional development with district staff on a monthly basis. He meets with first-grade teachers in his school every week. In regards to standards-based education, Mr. Quintana will arrange to

- discuss with district bilingual primary staff how the project illustrates a way for students to attain Goal 2, Standard 2

- compare with other first-grade teachers how bilingual students perform on their worksheets and bar graphs in relation to other students in bilingual and mainstream classes

FIGURE 2.21 FAMILY MEMBER CHECKLIST

First-Grade Bar Graph Project
(English version)

For the next 2 weeks, our class is learning how to measure objects. You can help by having your child arrange objects at home. Your child could use different size cans of food, different sizes of glasses or bottles, or other objects in your house. Ask your child to describe the objects to you in terms of size, shape, color, and height. Ask your child to compare the objects and talk about how tall and how short each one is.

At the end of the 2 weeks, your child is to make a graph that shows the heights of the persons in your household. We will make a graph at school that will show what your child is to do. On October 15, your child is to bring the graph to school. This checklist is to help you assist your child in the project. Please fill it out and send it with your child on that day.

For each activity, put an X to say YES, my child can do this, or NO, my child cannot do this. This information will be compared with other information from school. Thank you.

My child can	Yes	No
1. arrange objects from shortest to tallest.		
2. arrange objects from tallest to shortest.		
3. describe objects.		
4. compare objects by height.		
5. draw objects and write the number of objects drawn.		
6. arrange family members by height.		
7. make a graph that shows the relative heights of family members.		
8. write the names of family members on the graph.		
9. write the number next to the family member from the shortest to the tallest person.		

Child's name: _____

Name of family member: _____

PHASE 4: REPORTING AND DECISION MAKING

Student

Mr. Quintana reports results based on the evidence that has been collected, recorded, and analyzed during a conference with each student. Together, teacher and student set learning goals. For each student, during the course of this project, Mr. Quintana will (a) share the results of the task-specific checklist and (b) provide feedback from the teacher-student conference.

Family Members

At the beginning of the school year, family members are invited to the school's open house. Mr. Quintana has produced a video of a typical day in first grade during which the students narrate in Spanish and English what is happening. In addition, he shows family members

FIGURE 2.22 DISTRICT SUMMARY CHECKLIST

ESL Goal 2, Standard 2   To use English to achieve academically in all content areas: Students will use English to obtain, process, construct, and provide subject matter information in spoken and written form

Student: *Juan Carlos Moya*   Grade: *1*

Teacher: *Mr. Quintana*   School year: *2000*

School: _____   District: _____

Languages of instruction and assessment: *Spanish* (L1) *and English* (L2)

Directions: At the completion of each theme or project, place a check mark if the student consistently demonstrates attainment of the sample progress indicator (SPI) for the applicable content areas. Mark an X if the SPI has been addressed but the student has not yet demonstrated attainment. At the bottom of the page, provide the names of the curricular themes or projects. Use the corresponding numeral to identify the SPIs addressed in the theme or project. At the end of the year, based on accumulated evidence, determine if the student has or has not attained Goal 2, Standard 2.

Sample progress indicators	ESL	Math	Science	Social studies	Themes or projects
Identify and associate written symbols with words			X		1
Define, compare, and classify objects	✓				1
Record observations		X			1
Construct a graph showing data				X	1

Themes or projects:

1. *Bar graph project*

2. _____

3. _____

Attainment of Goal 2, Standard 2   Yes   No

---

examples of projects that students do throughout the year and emphasizes how important a role home and community play in the education of children. Student portfolios are on each student's desk and original student work is displayed. As other teachers at his school do, Mr. Quintana will

- hold conferences with parents at the end of the first quarter and show how Family Member Checklist has contributed to the assessment of the bar graph project

- inform family members of "Portfolio Night," when students come to school to share the contents of their portfolio

District Bilingual and Mainstream Teachers

Teachers throughout the district rely on multiple data sources to make decisions. One source of information is standardized tests. For ESL students, there are language proficiency tests in English (and Spanish) given on an annual basis. Students enrolled in the bilingual education program also take achievement tests in Spanish until they are at a point of transition into English. Classroom assessment that is referenced to ESL, district, and state standards complements these norm-referenced data. Mr. Quintana decides to

- meet with bilingual teachers from other grades to chart student progress

- share results of the classroom project with first-grade teachers and discuss links between ESL standards and the district's academic standards across content areas

- generate curricular ideas regarding the use of charts or graphs for depicting other data for other themes, such as weather conditions; students' birthdays each month; class surveys of favorite animals, foods, or colors; and size of the families of students in the class

Discussion and Reflection

This scenario illustrates how three distinct audiences have their own reasons for standards-based assessment and how, throughout the assessment cycle, each makes use of assessment information in different ways. In particular, family members are portrayed as active participants in the education of their children. Family members have an understanding of educational standards and are encouraged to use them in instruction and assessment of their children. Authentic instruction and assessment at home are built from the children's own experiences and reinforce learning from school.

As a bilingual teacher, proficient in Spanish, Mr. Quintana readily communicates with students and parents in their native language. In addition, he can access the rich resources of the Hispanic community. Parent volunteers assist in Mr. Quintana's classroom. By involving family members in the continuing education of their children, Mr. Quintana positively promotes the use of Spanish for academic support and honors the use of that language by parents. For example, the homework assignment using Family Member Checklist is provided in both Spanish and English.

Because Mr. Quintana uses a variety of manipulatives in his instructional plans, he often includes their use in his homework assignments. Mr. Quintana is well aware that many of his students' families do not have access to a wide range of material resources. When homework assignments require the use of special materials, he sends them home with students.

Although Mr. Quintana had designed Family Member Checklist as a way of structuring the graphing homework assignment, he found that many parents, both English and Spanish speaking, still had difficulty completing the task. Some of the families found the directions insufficient; others had had little experience with these kinds of academic tasks. He decides that, in the future, he will organize his homework assignments involving family members so that they build up from simpler to more complex assignments such as this one.

Mr. Quintana is able to coordinate services and articulate with other teachers regarding student attainment of ESL standards. The district has devised a summary checklist specifically for Goal 2, Standard 2, so that teachers will have a sense of the critical SPIs to be addressed and how that can be accomplished by integrating language and content. Furthermore, Mr. Quintana is a contributing member of a grade-level team that includes bilingual and classroom teachers. Teachers in this school district are afforded the opportunity for joint planning as part of a comprehensive professional development plan. In this way, standards-based assessment proceeds in a uniform and consistent manner across the district.

Connections

- There is a conscious connection or alignment between standards-based, classroom, and large-scale assessment. The rating scale for the bar graph project pertains to the specific theme or unit of study in the scenario, in this case, the measurement of objects. District Summary Checklist, on the other hand, uses the information gathered from themes throughout the year to determine to what extent Goal 2, Standard 2, has been attained.

- There is a blending of ESL standards with other academic content standards; here we see the ESL standards make a bridge to mathematics and social studies. Thus, the integration of language and content within an instructional setting is an effective instructional approach for these ESOL students.

- There is an understanding that standardized, norm-referenced data from tests (with proven validity) may be important for gauging the performance of ESOL students in relation to their peers at a national or state level. Information derived from performance assessment that is referenced to standards, however, is bound to be more closely aligned to curriculum and instruction at a district, school, program, or classroom level.

Goal 2, Standard 2, Grades 4–8

To use English to achieve academically in all content areas: Students will use English to obtain, process, construct, and provide subject matter information in spoken and written form

Sample Progress Indicators

- gather and organize the appropriate materials needed to complete a task
- record observations
- synthesize, analyze, and evaluate information
- participate in an academic activity and represent the sequence of events
- ask and answer authentic questions
- explain change

Context

Grade Level: Fourth-/fifth-grade mainstream class
English Proficiency Level(s): High beginning–high intermediate
Language(s) of Instruction: English
Focus of Instruction: Science and language arts
Location: Urban school district in the Southeast

Background

The scenario takes place in a mixed fourth-/fifth-grade classroom of 35 students from Cuba, the Dominican Republic, and Puerto Rico.[1] All of the students are speakers of English as a second language; 20 receive ESL instruction during the language arts block. The oral proficiency levels of the ESL students range from high beginning to high intermediate. Some of the students are just beginning to communicate in written text. The teacher, Mrs. Cornejo, is fluent in English and Spanish and certified in elementary education and ESL.

Five of the ESL students have also been identified as learning disabled. Because the school functions under an inclusion model, the regular classroom teacher receives assistance from both the ESL and special education teachers to support students' learning. The school's

---

[1] This scenario is not based on a vignette from *ESL Standards*.

multidisciplinary team, along with each student's parent, has developed an individualized educational plan (IEP) for each special education student. Both specialists (ESL and special education) provide one-to-one and small-group instruction in the regular classroom setting. They also conduct observations, offer suggestions, and provide assistance with informal assessment procedures. The regular classroom teacher is responsible for science instruction.

Allocation of Time

In science, the class is completing a unit on the water cycle. During the culminating lesson discussed in this vignette, the teacher is interested in the students' ability to conduct, discuss, and write about a science experiment: a simulation of a water cycle. This unit is composed of 10 lessons, each requiring 2–3 hours to complete. Some teachers introduce the reading and language development component first, while others begin with the hands-on activities and build in language development through students' experiences with the materials.

Instructional and Assessment Cycle

PHASE 1: PLANNING

The language arts component of each lesson introduces important vocabulary and specific ways of using language, such as asking questions, making reports, and organizing and planning. The science component builds students' concepts and understandings of science inquiry. The lessons are interdependent, developing students' understandings of science while promoting literacy and language use. The materials are designed to foster inquiry using student-generated authentic questions based on the National Science Education Standards (National Research Council, 1996). Initially, students are encouraged to communicate in either Spanish or English as they interact with the hands-on materials. At the completion of the activities, students are also encouraged to refine their thinking to provide more lengthy and precise oral and written communication.

The science unit contains pre- and posttests of students' science knowledge and written communication. The tests are correlated with the statewide assessment instruments for evaluating fourth-grade students' academic performance. In addition, the unit is designed so that the first lesson provides oral and written information on the students' understanding of the science content. Mrs. Cornejo uses this information to plan instruction, including ways to pace and review content, promote student interaction, and encourage individual students' participation and achievement. The last lesson is designed to provide a summary of students' understanding of the unit content and of their ability to engage in the inquiry process. Because many students are less familiar with science than with other subjects, Mrs. Cornejo is particularly interested in determining how much the students have learned.

Lessons 2–10 of the unit contain a similar organizational structure:

- development of an authentic inquiry question

- development of a plan for answering the question

- implementation of the plan

- data collection and analysis

- development of conclusions and explanations

- making oral and written reports of findings

The following chart (Figure 2.23) shows how assessment procedures are interwoven with the instructional activities for these lessons.

PHASE 2: COLLECTING AND RECORDING INFORMATION

As Figure 2.23 shows, Mrs. Cornejo uses a variety of assessment tools to collect information so that she is aware of students' needs and progress in the academic content. She has selected both formal and informal measures that include

- observation guides

- unit pre- and posttests correlated to state achievement tests

Figure 2.23 Aligning Sample Progress Indicators; Collecting and Recording Tools With Instructional Activities

Sample progress indicators	Instructional activity	Collection tools	Recording tools
• ask authentic questions	• develop inquiry questions	• students' logs	• students' portfolios
• answer authentic questions	• plan to answer question	• students' logs	• students' portfolios • teacher's grade book
• follow directions • gather and use materials • implement activity	• conduct science activity	• students' oral performance • collection and use of materials	• teacher observation guides
• record observations	• collect data	• tables and charts	• teacher's grade book
• analyze information	• analyze data	• oral discussions • graphs/drawings presenting information	• teacher's grade book
• synthesize and evaluate information	• prepare conclusions	• oral discussions • graphs/drawings presenting information	• teacher observation guides
• explain conclusions	• make oral and written reports	• oral discussions • informal written reports • formal written reports • videotapes of oral reports	• science reporting rubric • students' portfolios

- standard state assessment procedures at grade levels

- written reports

- specifically designed rubrics correlated to state achievement tests

- students' input and interactions

- observations of students' interactions

- students' written performance on identified activities

- videotapes of student performance

PHASE 3: ANALYZING AND INTERPRETING INFORMATION

As she collects information about students' performances, Mrs. Cornejo uses the information to promote instruction. She uses information on students' written and oral performance on unit activities to extend language and literacy development and science content learning. She monitors students' progress through the lessons and adjusts instruction to meet individual and group needs. She pays careful attention to students' ideas and understandings as well as to the linguistic forms and vocabulary used to communicate content. She uses the following plan for language and content:

- To check students' development of questions, Mrs. Cornejo observes students in class, provides models for framing questions, and helps students decide which questions are more relevant and appropriate to their interests. She encourages students to work together, to compare their questions, and to decide which ones would lead to the information they want. To foster ongoing self-assessment, Mrs. Cornejo encourages students to compare their questions across time by storing them in their science portfolios.

- To check students' plans for answering questions, Mrs. Cornejo encourages students to work together in forming inquiry plans. She fosters ongoing self-assessment of the planning activities through students' comparisons with previous work. At the end of the unit, she reviews the portfolios and discusses progress with the students.

- To check students' performance in conducting science activities, Mrs. Cornejo uses an observation guide she shares with the students. The observation guide (see Figure 2.24) focuses on students'
  — development of relevant inquiry questions
  — development of an inquiry plan
  — ability to develop and follow directions
  — performance in selecting, gathering, using, and storing materials
  — careful implementation of the activity

  Mrs. Cornejo discusses students' performances in terms of understanding the activity and anticipated outcomes.

FIGURE 2.24 OBSERVATION GUIDE FOR CONDUCTING SCIENCE ACTIVITIES

Name: _____ Date: _____

Directions: Based on your observation, place a check mark in the column to show that the student has performed each activity.

In this activity, the student

- developed relevant inquiry questions   _____

- developed an inquiry plan   _____

- developed and followed directions   _____

- selected materials   _____

- gathered materials   _____

- used materials   _____

- stored materials   _____

- implemented the activity   _____

- To check students' performance in collecting data, Mrs. Cornejo observes their interactions as well as their data collection charts and tables. After demonstrating data collection processes, she discusses grading criteria for their performance evaluation. She encourages students to see the relationship between the collection and interpretation of data. She records students' performance in collecting data in her grade book.

- To check students' performance in preparing conclusions, Mrs. Cornejo observes students' interactions, drafts of written summaries, and other evidence of academic performance. She encourages students' interactions in small groups to synthesize and evaluate their own and one another's performance. Because Mrs. Cornejo realizes that providing explanations and conclusions develops more slowly than other areas of the inquiry process, she uses the information to improve instruction and promote opportunities to learn. She does not use it for grading.

- To evaluate students' growth in making oral and written reports, Mrs. Cornejo creates a variety of response opportunities, such as writing letters to friends telling them what happened in the science lesson; making a videotape demonstrating the science activity; preparing formal written documents; and inviting the principal, parents, or other classes to attend lessons during which students give oral reports. For students who have not yet acquired the language to communicate understandings, they use drawings, tables, and graphs to support the reports. To evaluate students' progress, Mrs. Cornejo uses a science rubric that focuses on both the language and content of the report. She shares the rubric with students and parents and encourages its use in self-evaluation as well as ongoing language development.

PHASE 4: REPORTING AND DECISION MAKING

Mrs. Cornejo uses the information she collects to

- provide students, school administrators, and parents with feedback on students' progress

- identify specific instructional strengths and weaknesses

- provide opportunities for review and practice

- determine students' interests and strengths

- identify students' special instructional needs

MEETING THE INSTRUCTIONAL NEEDS OF SPECIAL EDUCATION STUDENTS

Although an understanding of students' language proficiency levels is important in meeting students' instructional needs, Mrs. Cornejo is aware that some students have learning needs beyond language proficiency in English. Mrs. Cornejo prepares a range of activities to accommodate multiple proficiency, performance, and ability levels. When working with students in small groups, she tailors her interactions to provide input at or slightly above students' proficiency levels. She organizes students in groups with different proficiency levels and encourages students to interact in ways that promote engagement and sharing. She uses activities that require students to make notes and pictures to indicate their understandings, communicate orally before writing, and review and evaluate their own and one another's work. Each of these strategies incorporates assessment into instruction.

In completing the unit, Mrs. Cornejo guides the class in a water cycle simulation, illustrating the cyclic process of evaporation, condensation, and precipitation. The activity consists of placing hot water in the bottom of a clear plastic cup, quickly covering it with a second inverted clear plastic cup, and placing a third clear plastic cup filled with ice on top. Students observe and discuss changes in the cups over time.

As she leads the class in completing the activity, Mrs. Cornejo focuses on a group of four students with different language proficiency levels. She is particularly interested in promoting communication with Ricardo, an inclusion student experiencing difficulty with learning language as well as science concepts. After Ricardo and his peers, Alejandro, Carla, and Evita, complete their group simulation, they discuss their observations. Next, they complete the three-step writing activity consisting of

1. listing the materials

2. writing the sequence of procedures

3. explaining the results

Ricardo tells the group which materials were used and writes brief statements indicating the first four steps in the procedures. Although he does not complete the task of explaining the results, he begins an explanatory paragraph about the activity. Mrs. Cornejo notices that Ricardo is focused on the task and participates in the oral discussion of the simulation. Mrs. Cornejo further notes that, with minimal assistance, Ricardo shows a clear understanding of the water cycle. Mrs. Cornejo is especially pleased to notice that after they complete the simulation, the students developed several inquiry questions to extend the simulation.

Discussion and Reflection

This scenario illustrates how assessment strategies are an essential part of the instructional process for both science and language arts. In meeting students' needs in general, by combining assessment with instruction, the teacher could (a) provide ongoing instruction that meets a variety of language and content-area requirements, (b) identify students' levels of language proficiency and use this information in instruction, (c) organize instructional groupings that promote social and academic interactions, and (d) use concrete materials to promote students' understanding of abstract concepts.

This scenario shows how the national science and ESL standards can be combined for effective instruction and assessment. The teacher is able to determine student progress on both sets of standards in a single instructional sequence.

The scenario also illustrates how students' special learning needs can be effectively met. For example, Mrs. Cornejo

- uses an established predictable format so that students can anticipate and follow the instructional process

- organizes groups with a range of language proficiencies so that students receive meaningful input for both language and content learning

- provides a supportive environment where students can use multiple communication modes (e.g., drawing, graphing) and multiple languages (e.g., English, Spanish) to contribute and achieve

- creates high yet realistic expectations, making students willing to engage in difficult tasks

Often students learning ESL and those with identified learning difficulties are excluded from cognitively and academically demanding instruction. This scenario illustrates the possibilities for making challenging instruction in academic areas (e.g., science) relevant for students with limited prior experience or opportunities to achieve.

Connections

This scenario also shows how IEPs can serve to facilitate standards-based instructional assessment for all students. IEPs can be written to incorporate standards within each student's plan and can thus allow teachers and district personnel to monitor attainment of standards.

Special education students are included in both classroom instruction and assessment activities. This scenario shows how special education students can be assessed using standards. It also highlights the importance of cooperation among mainstream, special education, and classroom teachers.

Goal 2, Standard 2, Grades 9–12, Advanced Level

To use English to achieve academically in all content areas: Students will use English to obtain, process, construct, and provide subject matter information in spoken and written form

Sample Progress Indicators

- locate information appropriate to an assignment in text or reference materials
- research information on academic topics from multiple sources
- take a position and support it orally or in writing
- prepare for and participate in a debate

Context

Grade Level: Eleventh-grade mainstream civics class
English Proficiency Level(s):   Advanced
Language(s) of Instruction: English
Focus of Instruction: Civics
Location: Urban school district in the Northeast

Background

The scenario takes place in an 11th-grade, one-semester civics course. Most of the 24 students in the class are of Hispanic background. Most ESOL students speak Spanish; other language groups include Haitian Creole and Chinese. Mr. Phillipe, the teacher, is certified in both civics and ESL. He is proficient in Haitian Creole and English and has a working knowledge of Spanish. Most of the students in this class are true advanced-level students, although some are more at the intermediate level. The students' ages range from 16 to 19. It is near the end of the school year.

Allocation of Time

This unit takes approximately 3 weeks. The first week is devoted to researching the topic and organizing the information. The following week centers on preparation and delivery of the debate, and the last week includes essay writing and reflection along with practicing for the departmental exam.

Instructional and Assessment Cycle

PHASE 1: PLANNING

Mr. Phillipe has planned a sequence of instructional activities around a unit on civic responsibility. According to this plan, students will

- collect articles from different sources on the topic

- talk about different ideas in six groups of four students

- record ideas on newsprint and share with the class

- develop a graphic organizer for ideas

- answer the teacher's questions as a group

- engage in a class discussion

- practice debating

- debate (some students debate, others prepare questions, and others critique)

- critique the debate

- write two essays, one discussing the debate and one focusing on a specific issue

- compile a list of references

Figure 2.25 shows the connections across SPIs, instructional activities for students, and assessment tools for collecting and recording information about students' performances.

PHASE 2: COLLECTING AND RECORDING INFORMATION

Mr. Phillipe has carefully chosen or designed assessment tools that will help him monitor students' progress across the tasks.

Doing the Research

So that students are prepared for the first step in the instructional plan, the class talks about various sources of information and spends a few class meetings in the media center (formerly known as a library), where they are introduced to and practice information searches. They become familiar with the following sources:

- newspapers

- magazines and journals

- encyclopedias

FIGURE 2.25 ALIGNING SAMPLE PROGRESS INDICATORS, INSTRUCTIONAL ACTIVITIES, AND ASSESSMENT

Sample progress indicators	Instructional activity	Collection tools	Recording tools
Locate information appropriate to an assignment in text or reference materials	Collect articles from different sources	Debate Information and Sources Inventory, Debate Sources Checklist	Debate Information and Sources Inventory, Debate Sources Checklist
Research information on academic topics from multiple sources	Collect articles from different sources; read and extract information	Debate Information and Sources Inventory, Debate Sources Checklist	Debate Information and Sources Inventory, Debate Sources Checklist
Take a position and support it orally or in writing	Engage in class discussion; debate; write essays	Debate Team Checklist, Departmental Writing Rubric	Debate Team Checklist, Departmental Writing Rubric
Prepare for and participate in a debate	Collect information; prepare for debate; debate	Debate Team Checklist	Debate Team Checklist

- other reference books
- text or trade books
- published videotapes
- original source documents
- personal interviews
- Web sites

The students also review the proper way to cite these sources in formal writing. As the class begins to collect articles and other sources of information, Mr. Phillipe decides to check on his students' progress in locating information to use in their debate and for their writing assignment. He wants them to use a variety of appropriate resources to show they know how to access information. To help students keep track of their resources in their journals, Mr. Phillipe provides students with an inventory form (Figure 2.26).

FIGURE 2.26 DEBATE INFORMATION AND SOURCES INVENTORY

Information	Name of source	Type of source

This inventory helps the students to organize the information for their debate and essays and to complete the part of the assignment that requires a list of references. It also allows Mr. Phillipe to determine efficiently if students are collecting the information they need and are drawing on multiple sources. Assessment is most useful if it is both efficient and informative. Mr. Phillipe only has to look through these forms to verify what he needs to know.

Mr. Phillipe also keeps track of the students' use of multiple sources by creating a simple form (Figure 2.27) that allows him to tally how many of the different kinds of sources the students have used based on their own records.

Mr. Phillipe puts a check mark for each unique source he finds listed in the students' notes and journals.

Preparing for the Debate

Mr. Phillipe divides the students into teams to prepare for a debate on one aspect of civic responsibility. Teams are chosen after the students have time to discuss the topic in small groups and form opinions. Students identify their own opinions and regroup into teams whose members' opinions differ in order to give the topic more objective treatment and teach the students to see issues from different points of view. Within each team, the students select three peers to present their team's position in the debate.

During the days before the debate, the class discusses the components of good arguments, effective delivery, and attitude. They devise a checklist (Figure 2.28) that the listeners can use to evaluate the debaters. Each box checked will be worth one point. This checklist allows the listeners to focus their attention and provides a basis for deciding who will win the debate.

The class scores both teams on the same form so that they can do a quick comparison. As the class members listen to the debate, they decide whether each criterion was met, and, if it was, they place a check mark under the corresponding team number.

FIGURE 2.27 DEBATE SOURCES CHECKLIST

Type of source	Number of examples
Newspapers	
Magazines and journals	
Encyclopedias	
Other reference books	
Text or trade books	
Published videotapes	
Original source documents	
Personal interviews	
Web sites	
Other	

FIGURE 2.28 DEBATE TEAM CHECKLIST

Item	Team 1	Team 2	Comments
The team's position on this topic was clear.			
The team provided research evidence that supported its position.			
The team's arguments were easy to follow.			
Team members spoke clearly to the audience.			
Team members effectively used appropriate vocabulary and different kinds of sentences to explain their arguments.			
The team's attitude was respectful but firm.			
Total Points			

Supporting a Position in Writing

Although not all students take sides in the debate, all must write an essay on their topic, choosing a position about it and then defending that position. This activity partially prepares them for the departmental end-of-course exam, which includes essay questions. The department uses a holistic scoring rubric, which is discussed with the students before they undertake their writing assignments to ensure expectations are clear. The rubric is on a 4-point scale, shown in Figure 2.29. A score of 3 meets the departmental standard. Mr. Phillipe records the assigned score at the bottom of the page. He may use an intermediate score, such as 2.5 or 3.5, if the student's work does not clearly fall into one level or another.

PHASE 3: ANALYZING AND INTERPRETING INFORMATION

The assessment instruments that Mr. Phillipe has integrated into the instructional sequence of activities lend themselves to rapid analysis.

Doing the Research

Mr. Phillipe can quickly glance at the inventory and checklist related to the research segment to monitor students' performance. This information allows Mr. Phillipe and his students to track their progress in doing the research. Using it, he can also show his department chair and the district curriculum director evidence that his ESOL students are meeting the part of the graduation standard that calls for researching topics using multiple sources of information.

Preparing for the Debate

After the debate, the class members tally their check marks to determine a winner. They give one point for each check mark. The debate team members are allowed to look at the unsigned checklists for detailed feedback about their performance.

FIGURE 2.29 DEPARTMENTAL WRITING RUBRIC

Student's name: _____

Topic: _____

Score	Description
4	The student shows command and in-depth knowledge of the topic. The student's position is clearly stated, logically developed, and strongly supported with several facts or citations of authoritative opinions. Facts are usually cited according to source. Opinions, including authoritative opinions, are clearly identified as such.
3	The student demonstrates knowledge of the subject and states a clear position. Most points are supported by citation of fact or authoritative opinion, sometimes by source. The student's position is clearly based on analysis of sources.
2	It is clear that the student has researched the topic and has some knowledge of it. The student's position is identifiable but not clearly based on cited fact or authoritative opinion. Some points appear to be opinion unsupported by researched sources.
1	The student demonstrates no identifiable position on the topic, or the position seems arbitrary and unsupported by research. Some sources may be cited but appear irrelevant to the points made.

Notes:

Score: _____

Supporting a Position in Writing

The notes section at the bottom of the rubric allows Mr. Phillipe to list specific examples to support the score he assigns. Because these students are also English language learners, he uses that block to make note of language patterns to bring to the student's attention or to address with the class if they appear in several students' work.

PHASE 4: REPORTING AND DECISION MAKING

Mr. Phillipe has used a variety of assessment instruments to collect and analyze information about students. He must now report information back to students and other stakeholders as well as use some results to make decisions.

Doing the Research

Mr. Phillipe has shared information with the department chair on students' ability to meet the graduation requirement for researching academic topics. Mr. Phillipe, after meeting with the department chair and his colleagues in the department, can now report to students how well they have progressed on this graduation requirement and also let them know areas in which they should improve.

Analyzing the Debate

Mr. Phillipe and the class will work together to provide feedback to the debate teams on their performance. Both the winning and losing teams can discuss with other class members the components of a successful debate. Mr. Phillipe may use some of the information gathered in the debate to help students target ways to improve their language proficiency. He may also encourage students who did not participate in the debate, especially ESOL students, to participate in the next debate or class presentation. He may also ask students to reflect on their progress in making oral presentations over the semester.

Reviewing the Writing Rubric

Mr. Phillipe will return the results of the writing assignment to students. He can work with students to compare their scores on this assignment with previous scores. He can also use the notes section to suggest improvements to students. The results of the writing assignment will be reported not only to students but also to parents, in the last set of parent conferences, and to the department, to demonstrate progress on the writing rubric.

Discussion and Reflection

This scenario shows the link between classroom and large-scale assessment. Mr. Phillipe includes some classroom assessments, including a peer checklist, with the writing assignment, which is a department-based task. This shows how Mr. Phillipe can gather a great deal of information for more than one purpose within a short-term topic. In addition, Mr. Phillipe also integrates some classroom assessment with large-scale department purposes. For example, he uses Debate Information and Sources Inventory, as well as Debate Sources Checklist, to provide information on student progress toward a graduation requirement. This is a good example of using one assessment activity to provide multiple kinds of information.

Mr. Phillipe also uses a cooperative teacher/student self-assessment instrument through the inventory. The inventory allows students to organize their sources while working with their instructor to ensure that they have collected a sufficient number of sources of information.

This scenario also demonstrates some effective ways to work with high intermediate- and advanced-level ESOL students. Though students at these proficiency levels may no longer receive ESL services, teachers and other staff can continue to provide support as students progress linguistically and academically.

Connections

- In this scenario, important sharing across levels occurs. Mr. Phillipe shares information on student progress with his department chair and colleagues. In turn, his department chair may be able to judge the students' ability to pass graduation requirements. The department chair can also use this information in district-level meetings, which will inform state-level meetings. These connections across levels are crucial in ensuring that ESOL students are included in graduation tests and can succeed on such tests.

- The scenario also shows how standards-based reporting forms are not difficult to develop. Mr. Phillipe has developed some of these forms for himself, though some could be developed by the department or district and shared with all teachers.

Goal 2, Standard 2, Grades 9–12, Beginning–Intermediate Level

To use English to achieve academically in all content areas: Students will use English to obtain, process, construct, and provide subject matter information in spoken and written form

Sample Progress Indicators

- locate information appropriate to an assignment in text or reference materials

- research information on academic topics from multiple sources

- take a position and support it orally or in writing

- prepare for and participate in a debate

Context

Grade Level:	Eleventh-grade sheltered civics class
English Proficiency Level(s):	Beginning–intermediate
Language(s) of Instruction:	English
Focus of Instruction:	Sheltered civics
Location:	Urban school district in the Northeast

Background

The scenario takes place in an 11th grade, one-semester sheltered civics course.[2] Students are from various backgrounds, including Spanish, Arabic, and Chinese. Ms. Habib, the teacher, is certified in both civics and ESL. She speaks some Arabic. Most of the students in this class are at the intermediate level; a few are at the beginning level. The students' ages range from 16 to 19. It is near the end of the school year.

---

[2] This scenario is similar to the scenario for Goal 2, Standard 2, Grades 9–12, featuring Mr. Phillipe but has been modified for a group of students at a lower level of English language proficiency. Note that some of the text is the same for both scenarios and several instruments are used in both.

Allocation of Time

There are three segments within this instructional unit. Each segment of this unit will require approximately 7 class days, or about 4 weeks total.

Instructional and Assessment Cycle

PHASE 1: PLANNING

Ms. Habib has planned a sequence of instructional activities around a unit on civic responsibility. Because students are at lower levels of English language proficiency, Ms. Habib has carefully structured appropriate activities for students at these levels to lead up to a class debate and individual student essays. Ms. Habib monitors students' progress in completing these tasks, in large part by weaving in a series of journal writing assignments. According to her plan, students will

- explore ideas related to civic responsibility by discussing them in a variety of activity groups

- expand their knowledge base by collecting articles from different sources on the topic and interviewing experts in those areas

- express their ideas through formal language structures such as debate and essay writing

PHASE 2: COLLECTING AND RECORDING INFORMATION

Exploring Ideas

To guide students as they brainstorm ideas on civic responsibility, Ms. Habib has prepared a list of questions for the class to discuss. They include:

- What are the problems around this civic responsibility (e.g., keeping public parks clean and safe)?

- How long have these problems existed?

- What are the effects?

- Who is affected the most?

- What will happen if nothing is done?

- What are causes of these problems?

- What are the debates around these issues?

After engaging in the brainstorming activity, students complete a journal writing entry in response to this prompt: "What I understand about the issues around (e.g., keeping parks clean and safe). . . ."

Next, Ms. Habib puts students in groups of three or four according to the civic responsibilities they wish to work on. Each group narrows its topic, using Graphic Organizer A (Figure 2.30). For example, the students may have decided that volunteering to help children

FIGURE 2.30 GRAPHIC ORGANIZER A

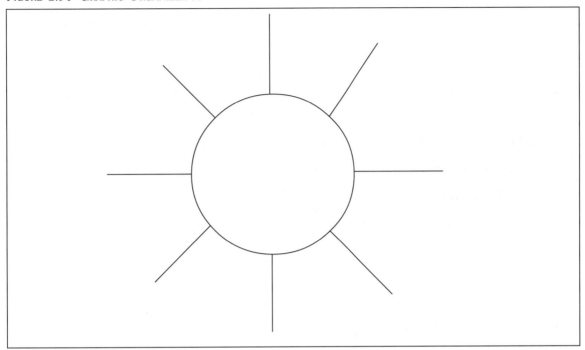

in the community was the responsibility they wanted to study. The graphic organizer helps them narrow their topic to helping homeless children, reading to elementary school children, and so forth.

To focus their research, students need to decide what they need to find out and assign collection of information to different members of the group. Ms. Habib provides the groups with Graphic Organizer B (Figure 2.31) to help them with this task.

FIGURE 2.31 GRAPHIC ORGANIZER B

Topic:_____

What I already know	What I need to know/What I want to know

Expanding Knowledge Base

Ms. Habib leads a discussion on various sources of information, and students take notes on research vocabulary related to library searches, on-line searches, expert interviews, and other sources of information using Graphic Organizer C in Figure 2.32.

Ms. Habib helps her students identify experts in the community to assist them in their research. For expert interviews, Ms. Habib provides them with this checklist:

Make an appointment with the expert. _____

Decide how to dress and act appropriately. _____

Role-play the interview with a partner. _____

Write questions to be covered. _____

Take notes. _____

Send a written thank-you note. _____

After conducting the interviews, students complete a journal writing entry in response to this prompt: "My thoughts and feelings about my interview with. . . ."

Ms. Habib then asks the students to report the information they have collected using Debate Information and Sources Inventory (Figure 2.26). As the second part of this task, she asks that they paraphrase the information that they have previously collected. Ms. Habib uses a four-step modeling process to teach paraphrasing:

1. First, I show you. You watch and listen.

2. Next, I show you and you help me.

FIGURE 2.32 GRAPHIC ORGANIZER C

Note think	Note talk	Note review
(Write main points here when you review and study.)	(Take notes here.)	(Put graphic organizers here to help you relate new material to what you already know and to organize your thoughts.)

3. Then, you show me and I help you.

4. Finally, you do the task alone.

Expressing Ideas Through Formal Language Structures

To prepare students for the debate, Ms. Habib shows several videotaped debates. The social studies department has a small library of such debates, including several past presidential debates as well as debates among local candidates. Students then use Debate Team Checklist (see Figure 2.28) to analyze the debate participants they saw on the videos. Students complete this writing assignment for their journals by responding to the following prompt: "What I understand about debates. . . ."

In groups, students predict the arguments that may be used against them. They begin to organize and prepare their arguments for the class debate. In their teams, they role-play and practice presenting the opposing arguments they have already predicted will be used.

Students conduct the debate in teams. After each debate, the class members evaluate the debate teams' performances, again using Debate Team Checklist. They then complete a writing assignment for their journals by responding to the following prompt: "What I learned about the issues included. . . ."

The culminating activity for this unit is for students to support their position in writing. To make sure students understand the criteria by which their writing will be assessed, Ms. Habib gives each student a copy of Departmental Writing Rubric (Figure 2.29). Students examine examples of student writing to help them see what a 4 or a 3 paper looks like.

Ms. Habib also gives the students a copy of Graphic Organizer D (Figure 2.33) as a prewriting step to help them organize their ideas. Students review the steps of the writing process and begin to write their rough draft of their individual essays, using their notes and Venn diagrams.

FIGURE 2.33 GRAPHIC ORGANIZER D

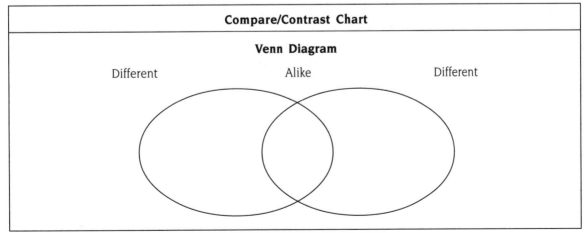

PHASE 3: ANALYZING AND INTERPRETING INFORMATION

The assessment instruments that Ms. Habib has integrated into the instructional sequence of activities lend themselves to quick analysis.

Exploring Ideas

Ms. Habib reviews students' journals and completed graphic organizers to monitor students' engagement in the brainstorming and exploration activities and their progress in selecting a focus for inquiry.

Expanding Knowledge Base

Ms. Habib quickly checks the inventory and checklist related to the research segment to track the students' progress in doing the research. Using them, she can also show her department chair and the district curriculum director evidence that her ESOL students are meeting the part of the graduation standard that calls for researching topics by locating and using multiple sources of information.

Expressing Ideas Through Formal Language Structures

After using Debate Team Checklist, both for critiquing the videotaped debates and their classmates' debates, class members tally their check marks to determine a winner. They give one point for each check mark. To provide feedback to student debate team members, classmates give debate team members an opportunity to look at the unsigned checklists for detailed feedback about their performance.

Students' essays are scored using a departmental scoring rubric. The notes block at the bottom of the rubric allows Ms. Habib to list specific examples to support the score she assigns. Because these students are ESOL students, she uses that block to make note of language patterns to bring to the student's attention or to address with the class if they appear in several students' work.

PHASE 4: REPORTING AND DECISION MAKING

Ms. Habib has used a variety of assessment instruments to collect and analyze information about students. She must now report information back to students and other stakeholders as well as use some results to make decisions.

Feedback to Students

Ms. Habib reads students' journal entries and makes brief comments on their progress across the various activities within this unit. Students also receive feedback from one another as they engage in group activities and review Debate Team Checklists filled in by classmates. Students receive feedback on their essays via the departmental scoring rubric. In a conference with each student, Ms. Habib works with the student to compare his or her scores on this assignment with previous scores. They also discuss the notes section to focus on areas for improvement.

Feedback to the Department

Ms. Habib meets with the department chair and her colleagues in the department to discuss the progress of her students in meeting graduation requirements.

Feedback to Ms. Habib

After reading the journal entries, Ms. Habib discovered that this class of students found that conducting interviews with experts was problematic because of both language and cultural issues. They found that their low English language proficiency made it difficult to collect the needed information. In addition, some students found it culturally inappropriate to ask pointed questions of older and respected members of the community. Ms. Habib decides to modify the assignment so that students are better prepared to conduct these interviews.

Discussion and Reflection

This scenario highlights the ways in which a lesson can be modified to support the learning of students at lower levels of English language proficiency, especially through the use of graphic organizers. It reminds us that we need to provide all students with challenging academic content, even as they are acquiring language foundations.

Connections

This scenario illustrates the need for teachers and other educational professionals to expand their thinking about who constitutes a community leader. It may have been easier in this scenario for students to interview leaders within their own cultural groups who may not, in a U.S. context, occupy leadership positions but who are recognized as leaders in that community. A civics lesson is a superb opportunity to address these kinds of cross-cultural civics issues. This scenario highlights the need to rethink and restructure our lessons so that they mirror the cultural contexts from which our students come.

Goal 2, Standard 3, Grades 9–12

To use English to achieve academically in all content areas: Students will use appropriate learning strategies to construct and apply academic language

Sample Progress Indicators

- seek out print and nonprint resources in the native language when needed
- verbalize relationships between new information and information previously learned
- take notes to summarize the main points provided in source material
- practice an oral report with a peer prior to presenting it in class
- seek out more knowledgeable others (e.g., peers, teachers) with whom to consult to advance understanding

Context

Grade Level: Ninth- to 11th-grade, nongraded, regular math class
English Proficiency Level(s):   Beginning
Language(s) of Instruction: English
Focus of Instruction: Consumer math
Location: Rural school district in the Southwest

Background

The scenario takes place in a high school consumer math class, midway through the school year, in a rural school district. In addition to math skills, study skills and problem-solving strategies are part of the curriculum. The teacher, Mr. Jones, is a monolingual English speaker with minimal training in working with ESOL students. However, he has arranged to collaborate with the ESL teacher who is proficient in Spanish to monitor the progress of the ESOL students in his classroom. Most of the students are non-ESOL students spanning Grades 9–11. Three ESOL students, recently arrived from Mexico, attend the class.

Allocation of Time

This series of instructional activities and assessments is approximately 3 weeks in duration. The first week is devoted to review and selection of appropriate strategies for the project. In

Week 2, the ESOL students use the selected strategies to prepare for and practice presentations for the consumer math class on the geometry of structures. Working as a group, the three ESOL students decide to focus on how to construct a tool shed. Week 3 focuses on the presentation and reflection on the strategies used.

Instructional and Assessment Cycle

PHASE 1: PLANNING

Mr. Jones collaborates with the ESL teacher to plan a sequence of instructional activities to help the ESOL students use learning strategies to prepare presentations. They decide on the following instructional sequence:

1. Mr. Jones will guide the class through a review of strategies learned throughout the semester.

2. All students will use the review to brainstorm possible strategies to prepare for a presentation. Based on the review and brainstorming, ESOL students will

   - gather ideas in Spanish on how to construct a tool shed by brainstorming what they already know and by talking with parents or friends knowledgeable about the topic

   - meet with Mr. Jones to review the topic and clarify their understanding of the assignment

   - meet with the ESL teacher or one another to clarify any unknown vocabulary

   - revise notes and write notes in English on note cards to structure their presentation

3. All students will practice presentations with peers and incorporate feedback.

4. Students will conduct presentations.

5. Students will review and reflect on preparation and performance and evaluate strategies used.

6. Students will discuss other uses for these strategies in math class with classmates and Mr. Jones.

After reviewing the instructional goals and activities, Mr. Jones reflects on how he can monitor his students' progress by developing specific assessment activities that reflect the goals of the assignment. Figure 2.34 outlines his assessment plan.

Next, Mr. Jones selects collection and recording tools that correspond to the instructional activities and ways to analyze the information collected. He works with the ESL teacher to develop a self-assessment tool (Figure 2.35), which the ESL teacher translates into Spanish for use by the beginning ESOL students. Finally, he sketches how the results will be shared with students and other stakeholders.

FIGURE 2.34 PURPOSES FOR ASSESSMENT

Student	1. Monitor progress toward achieving sample progress indicators:
	  (a) student's progress in seeking out nonprint resources in the native language when needed
	  (b) student's progress in verbalizing relationships between new information and information previously learned in other settings
	  (c) student's progress in seeking more knowledgeable others with whom to consult to advance understanding of a concept or skill
	  (d) student's progress in practicing an oral report with a peer prior to presenting it
	  (e) student's progress in taking notes from sources
	2. Assess ability to work independently and manage time.
	3. Assess ability to self-evaluate and monitor learning.

Teacher	1. Determine effectiveness of collaboration with ESL teacher. 2. Assess effectiveness/appropriateness of activities in instructional sequence. 3. Assess effectiveness/appropriateness of collection/assessment tools.
ESL teacher	1. Determine effectiveness of collaboration with content-area teacher.

PHASE 2: COLLECTING AND RECORDING INFORMATION

Mr. Jones, in collaboration with the ESL teacher, collects and records assessment information as ESOL students participate in the planned instructional activities. Mr. Jones integrates the assessments into the instruction.

- Using Learning Log/Self-Assessment Form, which students can complete in either Spanish or English, the students keep track of and reflect on the strategies used to prepare for the presentations and assess the success of the strategies. Mr. Jones also uses this form to assess students' ability to reflect on strategy use.

- Using an observation note sheet (see Figure 2.36), Mr. Jones and the ESL teacher observe students and take notes on their use of the strategies.

- Using his record book, Mr. Jones and the students meet on two occasions to monitor students' management of time for the project.

The following chart (Figure 2.37) shows how Mr. Jones will align collection and reporting tools with specific purposes for assessment.

PHASE 3: ANALYZING AND INTERPRETING INFORMATION

As he collects information about ESOL students' progress, Mr. Jones and the ESL teacher analyze the information so that they can adjust instruction and provide feedback.

- To check on his ESOL students' use of strategies, Mr. Jones, collaborating with the ESL teacher, reviews students' reflections on Learning Logs/Self-Assessment Forms. They compare students' perceptions of their strategy use on this task with those from a prior task to assess progress in strategies use. They also look at comments on the observation note sheet related to how students use strategies to determine effectiveness of strategies used. In addition, they consider students' comments on the log and

FIGURE 2.35 LEARNING LOG/SELF-ASSESSMENT FORM (ENGLISH VERSION)*

Directions: Keep a record of the strategies used over the course of the project. As you use a strategy, take notes on what you did, how the strategy helped you, and when you would use the strategy again. At the completion of the project, evaluate your use of learning strategies by answering the final two questions.

As you prepare your project

Name of strategy	When/how did you use the strategy to accomplish the task?	Did the strategy help you prepare for the speech? How did it help you? Why didn't it help you?	When would you use the strategy again?
Use native language resources	I used Spanish to gather my ideas at the beginning of the project. I wrote my notes in Spanish, and I talked to my father and uncle in Spanish about construction.	The strategy helped me because I was able to get a lot more information for the speech. I was able to talk to people who do not speak English well.	I would use this strategy again for another presentation or project when I knew that I had resources in Spanish.
Use what I know to learn something new			
Take notes			
Practice presentation with a peer			
Talk to more knowledgeable people about the subject			

After you present

1. How would you rate your presentation?   Excellent   Good   Fair   Poor

2. Did using learning strategies help you make a better presentation than you would have otherwise?

   Definitely   Somewhat   Not at all

   If so, which ones?

3. What other strategies might you use next time for this project?

Note. * ESOL students received the Spanish version of this form.

FIGURE 2.36 TEACHER OBSERVATION NOTE SHEET

Directions: Use the observation note sheet to take notes on the strategies a student uses. Include notes on strategies that you see the student use or that you hear the student talk about in meetings.

Student's name _____

Strategy observed/mentioned	Notes/dates
Use what you know to learn something new	
Take notes	
Practice presentation with a peer	
Talk to more knowledgeable people about the subject	

teacher comments on the note sheet about ESOL students' use of strategies in relation to the strategies used by native-English-speaking peers. In this way, Mr. Jones and the ESL teacher can identify possible gaps in ESOL students' use of strategies.

- To check on ESOL students' ability to self-evaluate, Mr. Jones reviews the observation note sheets. With the ESL teacher, he reviews Learning Logs/Self-Assessment Forms to see if students' self-evaluations correspond to his assessment of students' use of strategies and to the ESL teacher's assessment. With the ESL teacher, he also reads students' learning logs to determine the degree to which students can reflect on their own learning.

FIGURE 2.37 ALIGNING ASSESSMENT PURPOSES WITH COLLECTING AND REPORTING TOOLS

Purpose	Collection tools	Reporting tools
Monitor student's progress in using the selected strategies	Observation note sheet, self-assessment form	Student conference, results of observation note sheets
Assess student's ability to self-evaluate	Observation note sheet, self-assessment form	Student conference, results of observation note sheets
Assess student's ability to manage time	Teacher record book	Student conference
Assess effectiveness of instructional and assessment tools	Observation note sheet, self-assessment form	Student conference, results of observation note sheets

- To assess his students' ability to manage their time, Mr. Jones meets twice with each ESOL student. During the meetings, he records their progress on the project. Later, Mr. Jones compares students' record sheets to determine which students will need additional help in managing their time.

- To determine the effectiveness of instruction, Mr. Jones keeps track of ESOL students' progress with strategies over the year by reading student comments in their learning logs, listening to comments in posttask discussions, and reviewing comments on the teacher observation note sheets. When a student has difficulty using a strategy effectively, Mr. Jones reviews that strategy with the student. Quarterly, Mr. Jones asks all students to evaluate the effectiveness of strategies instruction with a questionnaire.

- To determine the effectiveness of the instruments, Mr. Jones reviews the data collected from the various instruments in relation to his intended purposes.

PHASE 4: REPORTING AND DECISION MAKING

Mr. Jones uses the information he has collected on his ESOL students' use of learning strategies in several ways:

- Mr. Jones comments on the Learning Logs/Self-Assessment Forms and returns them to each student. The student includes the form, along with other documentation from the project, in his or her portfolio.

- Mr. Jones reviews the teacher observation note sheet with each student.

- Based on comments from the ESL teacher on the observation sheets, Mr. Jones and the ESL teacher decide that they need to review the strategy of taking notes with the students.

- Based on students' comments from the posttask discussion, Mr. Jones decides that he is going to give all students more opportunities to practice and discuss learning strategies in class.

Discussion and Reflection

This scenario shows how Mr. Jones

- attends to a variety of assessment purposes, including monitoring student learning, teacher instruction, and collaborative relationships

- includes students in instruction and assessment activities, including assessing instruction

- plans assessment along with instruction to ensure that he is helping students monitor progress toward preestablished goals and objectives

Teaching learning strategies requires ongoing assessment by the teacher and students for development of appropriate and successful use of those strategies. Students need practice using, assessing, and discussing strategies to learn how and when to use them to improve performance on academic tasks. By reflecting on and evaluating their use of strategies consistently, students will become more conscious of and more self-directed in their learning.

This scenario illustrates the importance of primary language support for beginning-level students so that they can have access to curricular goals. It also shows that although providing this access is rewarding, it requires additional resources.

In addition, the scenario demonstrates how students can use learning strategies in their native language as well as in English. As the ESOL students in this scenario are still more proficient in Spanish, they benefit from the opportunities to acquire learning strategies in Spanish. Later, these strategies readily transfer to English.

Connections

- Because ESOL students comprise such a small proportion of students in this class, Mr. Jones decides to collect their work and put it into portfolios so that he can monitor progress over time. This collection is particularly important because the work these students produce is more difficult to assess using the mainstream tools available to Mr. Jones. Note that Mr. Jones and the ESL teacher build these portfolios collaboratively to form a clearer picture of student achievement. These portfolios, then, provide a basis for communication about student achievement grounded in actual student work and measured against ESL standards.

- Within this math class, Mr. Jones creates opportunities to teach students how to utilize learning strategies to enhance their learning of math.

- Based on this successful collaboration, Mr. Jones, the ESL teacher, and some other teachers in the school meet to discuss future ways to collaborate within the school.

Goal 3, Standard 1, Program Manager Version

To use English in socially and culturally appropriate ways: Students will use the appropriate language variety, register, and genre according to audience, purpose, and setting

Program Manager Version

Because this scenario is geared to the needs of program managers, it is not set within a classroom vignette.[3] Instead, it shows how a standards-based instructional sequence can be established at a range of grade levels within a program.

Sample Progress Indicators

GRADES PRE-K–3 INDICATORS

- interact with an adult in formal and informal settings
- make polite requests*
- write a letter or e-mail to an adult using appropriate forms*
- demonstrate ways to show gratitude (e.g., write a follow-up letter)

GRADES 4–8 INDICATORS

- advise peers on appropriate language use*
- write business* and personal letters
- use idiomatic speech appropriately
- make polite requests*
- write a letter or e-mail to an adult using appropriate forms*
- demonstrate ways to show gratitude (e.g., write a follow-up letter)

GRADES 9–12 INDICATORS

- see the appropriate register for business* and friendly transactions
- write business* and personal letters

[3] We are using *program manager* as a generic term to include project director, program coordinator, district administrator, and so forth.

- use idiomatic speech appropriately

- advise peers on appropriate language use*

- make polite requests

- write a letter or e-mail to an adult using appropriate forms*

- demonstrate ways to show gratitude (e.g., write a follow-up letter)

Note: Indicators with an asterisk are specifically incorporated into the description of this instructional and assessment sequence. Others could be easily incorporated or could be part of a subsequent instructional sequence.

Context

Grade Level: First–12th grade
English Proficiency Level(s): Limited formal schooling–advanced ESL
Language(s) of Instruction: English
Focus of Instruction: The traits of *voice* and *word choice* from a six-trait model for writing instruction
Location: Urban district in the Northwest

Background

STATE CONTEXT

The state has developed Essential Learnings in Reading, Writing, and Communication. State tests at Grades 4, 7, and 10 measure student proficiency on these Essential Learnings. A Certificate of Mastery (10th-grade test) will be required for graduation. Only ESOL students who have been in school where the language of instruction is English for less than 1 year may be exempted from these tests.

DISTRICT CONTEXT

The district has grade-level content standards that relate to the state Essential Learnings (i.e., the content standards describe what the outcome looks like for students of different ages). The district has developed assessments for the reading content standards and uses a six-trait model to assess student development in writing. The state assessment for writing is based on the same underlying premise as the six-trait model but groups the trait into two large categories. Thus, the two assessments are in alignment.

ESL PROGRAM CONTEXT

The ESL program has developed ESL content standards that reflect the district-level content standards and incorporate the ESL standards. The district content standards and the SPIs (e.g., write business and personal letters) are the same in Grades 7–12. For Grades K–6, the district content standards and TESOL indicators vary, but the focus is still appropriate use of language according to the audience and situation. Although the outcome of the instruction described in the scenario is a written product, appropriate oral language usage is also incorporated into the instructional sequence.

CLASSROOM CONTEXT

Classrooms are ESL classes in Grades 1–12, and all students in the classes are ESOL students. All teachers are ESL endorsed; some speak languages other than English, but English is the language of instruction. In the newcomer and limited formal schooling (LFS) classrooms, bilingual assistants provide L1 support for 7 of the 42 languages spoken in the district.

RATIONALE FOR THE CHOICE OF ACTIVITY

The district has determined the importance of formal writing for all students in the district, and teachers have selected some important traits of language use. *Voice* and *word choice* are related to appropriate use of language according to audience and purpose. These traits are taught as part of the required instructional sequence in the district. The instructional model encourages and supports student reflection about appropriate language use. It also encourages peer interaction, thus increasing opportunities for oral language development, and links all four modes of language.

The rationale for using the six-trait model is built on a close link between instruction and assessment. Students are taught the criteria for assessment as they learn each trait and are taught to evaluate their own and peers' work according to these criteria. The skill with which this can be accomplished varies greatly according to grade level and level of English proficiency, but the process is the same.

Allocation of Time

This instruction and assessment cycle will take 3 weeks, although time allotment will vary with grade and proficiency level. This scenario assumes that instruction in the writing process per se has occurred earlier in the year and that students are accustomed to working through the steps of the process at a level of independence commensurate with their age and proficiency in English. The scenario also assumes that students have had an introduction to the traits of voice and word choice and have seen these traits modeled through literature and group reading.

WEEK 1

Students review traits of voice and word choice by (a) listening to models of effective word choice, (b) comparing effective and noneffective spoken and written communication, (c) brainstorming appropriate word choices, and (d) examining voice in different contexts. Some students and classes may begin prewriting activities. Younger students and LFS students may be led through prewriting activities by their instructor.

WEEK 2

Students begin to draft and revise according to the pace appropriate for their age and proficiency level. For primary and LFS students, the actual writing may be a group project led by the teacher. The product for these students may be a class letter or a letter that varies only in the specific request from each student.

WEEK 3

Some students may need to continue revising. Students edit, publish, and send letters.

Instructional and Assessment Cycle

PHASE 1: PLANNING

By this point in the year, students have already received instruction in and experience with the following:

- experience in writing personal letters

- instruction in the steps of the writing process

- introduction to the concept of traits of writing, specifically to the traits of voice and word choice

- some experience in rating their own and others' papers (note: the six-trait model does not recommend formal application of the rating standards for students below third grade; however, the process and underlying concepts may be used effectively in instruction)

The length of time for each step in the following sequence of activities will vary according to age and level of proficiency of the students:

1. State the objective for the unit, namely, writing business letters. The specific purpose of the letter is to gather information that the students can use in a content-area lesson.

2. Review the steps of the writing process.

3. Review students' previous experience with voice and word choice.

4. Share models of effective and ineffective business letters with the class.

5. For prewriting, have the students decide what they want to ask about in their letters. They can use various prewriting techniques (e.g., brainstorming, webs, reading) to develop word banks.

6. For drafting, have students (or the class in case of LFS and newcomers) write a first draft.

7. For revising, have students first revise alone and then with peers or in groups (again, depending on age and level of proficiency). They should begin to revise letters by examining word choice and voice. At various grades and levels of proficiency, students will look for the following:
   - slang versus standard English
   - abbreviations versus fully spelled words

- formal versus informal language (e.g., *thanks* or *thank you*)

- specific versus generic language (e.g., *I want information about Alaska* or *I want a list of the national parks in Alaska*)

- the form of the letter or e-mail (e.g., heading, closing)

- the politeness of the letter (e.g., standard formulaic language to express polite requests)

8. For editing, have students edit letters looking for other traits, such as ideas, organization, and conventions (i.e., grammar, capitalization, spelling). The focus of the exercise remains the traits of voice and word choice.

9. Publish and send letters or e-mails.

10. If desired, give older or more proficient students the opportunity to compare the form of a business letter with that of an e-mail letter.

Figure 2.38 provides an overview of the assessment plan.

PHASE 2: COLLECTING AND RECORDING INFORMATION

Assessment of Students' Progress in Producing Targeted Language Outcomes

Students will write or e-mail a business letter requesting specific information on a topic from a teacher, business, school, or government agency or university. The actual form and content of students' letters will vary by grade or level of English proficiency.

Assessment of Students' Use of the Writing Process

Students at all levels are taught to keep writing folders, which contain evidence of each step of the process, from prewriting through final product. Depending on grade level and level of students' English proficiency, teachers may

- audit folders, providing feedback to students (e.g., either orally or through the use of written comments on a checklist)

- record participation as the group moves through each step (e.g., primary and LFS students will do prewriting together and some drafting as a group; finished products

FIGURE 2.38 PURPOSES FOR ASSESSMENT

Student	• Achieve progress toward content standard/sample progress indicator • Achieve progress toward state test for Grades 4, 7, or 10 • Acquire a useful/relevant life skill • Develop metacognitive skills that will help in monitoring language production for other purposes • Follow steps of the writing process: prewriting, drafting, revising, editing, and publishing
Teacher	• Assess the effectiveness of instruction
ESL department	• Note the need for materials (e.g., models of good writing) and/or training • Assess ESOL students' progress toward district/state standards

may have the same general framework varying only in the specific information one student requests)

To determine students' success in performing these tasks, teachers will use a consistent set of criteria. Whereas specific rubrics will vary by grade or level of English proficiency, each will document how well

- students follow all steps of the writing process

- students write letters (or e-mails) that reflect appropriate voice and word choice for business letters

- students who are unable to write demonstrate orally that they are aware of appropriate language for making polite, formal requests

PHASE 3: ANALYZING AND INTERPRETING INFORMATION

For students in Grades 4 and above, letters will be rated on a 5-point scale for the traits of word choice and voice. Letters will be rated by the author, at least one peer, and the teacher. If this is the activity selected for the annual district Six-Trait Rating Scale (Figure 2.39), random papers from each class will also be rated by other teachers in the school or on the districtwide rating team.

For students in Grades K–3 and LFS students, the letters will not be formally rated on the 5-point scale but will be compared to benchmark papers from students of similar age groups and levels of proficiency.

PHASE 4: REPORTING AND DECISION MAKING

In Grades 4 and above, after the letters have been rated by the student, a peer, and the teacher, teachers enter the results of the three raters on a comprehensive rating sheet (Figure 2.40). Note that this rating sheet could be used for either oral or written assessment.

Discussion and Reflection

This scenario is complex because it is written from a program-level perspective rather than an individual classroom perspective. It does, however, illustrate ways in which the ESL goals and standards can be used, such as to

- link appropriate goals for ESOL students to district or state requirements for all students

- link language development across content areas and language modes

- provide a continuum of language development across grade and proficiency levels

- help students evaluate their own progress on this continuum

This scenario also helps teachers and district personnel identify students' strengths and weaknesses in producing formal writing. It will help all personnel plan for student readiness in large-scale assessment.

FIGURE 2.39 SIX-TRAIT RATING SCALE

	1	3	5
Ideas and content	As yet, the paper has no clear sense of purpose or central theme. To extract meaning from the text, the reader must make inferences based on sketchy details. The writing reflects more than one problem (e.g., information is very limited or unclear).	The writer is beginning to define the topic, even though development is still basic or general.	This paper is clear and focused. It holds the reader's attention. Relevant anecdotes and details enrich the central theme or story line.
Organization	The writing lacks a clear sense of direction. Ideas, details, or events seem strung together in a loose or random fashion—or else there is no identifiable internal structure. The writing reflects more than one problem (e.g., sequencing needs work).	The organizational structure is strong enough to move the reader through the text without undue confusion.	The organization enhances and showcases the central idea or story line. The order, structure, or presentation of information is compelling and moves the reader through the text.
Voice	The writer seems indifferent, uninvolved, or distanced from the topic or the audience. As a result, the writing is lifeless or mechanical. Depending on the topic, the writing may be overly technical or jargonistic. The paper reflects more than one problem (e.g., it is hard to sense the writer behind the words).	The writer seems sincere but not fully engaged or involved. The result is pleasant or even personable but not compelling.	The writer speaks directly to the reader in a way that is individualistic, expressive, and engaging. Clearly, the writer is involved in the text, is sensitive to the needs of an audience, and is writing to be read.
Word choice	The writer struggles with a limited vocabulary, searching for words to convey meaning. The writing reflects more than one problem (e.g., words are used incorrectly, sometimes making the message hard to decipher).	The language is functional, even if it lacks punch; it is easy to figure out the writer's meaning on a general level.	Words convey the intended message in a precise, interesting, and natural way.

Continued on page 98

FIGURE 2.39 SIX-TRAIT RATING SCALE (CONTINUED)

	1	3	5
Sentence fluency	The reader has to practice quite a bit to give this paper a fair interpretive reading. The writing reflects more than one problem (e.g., sentences are choppy, incomplete, rambling, or awkward).	The text hums along with a steady beat but tends to be more pleasant or businesslike than musical and more mechanical than fluid.	The writing has an easy flow and rhythm when read aloud. Sentences are well built, with strong and varied structure that invites expressive oral reading.
Conventions	Errors in spelling, punctuation, usage and grammar, capitalization, and paragraphing repeatedly distract the reader and make the text difficult to read. The writing reflects more than one problem (e.g., errors in grammar or usage are very noticeable and may affect meaning).	The writer shows reasonable control over a limited range of standard writing conventions. Conventions are sometimes handled well and enhance readability; at other times, errors are distracting and impair readability.	The writer demonstrates a good grasp of standard writing conventions and uses conventions effectively to enhance readability. Errors tend to be so few and so minor that the reader can easily overlook them unless hunting for them specifically.

As noted previously, students, peers, and teachers all use the same rubric for writing assessment at the classroom level. When scores are to be reported at the district level, other teachers or members of the district rating team score the papers as well. Raters must reach consensus regarding student performance on a scale of 1–5. This provision for interrater agreement ensures the reliability of the assessment.

FIGURE 2.40 RATING SHEET FOR ORAL OR WRITTEN ASSESSMENT

Student name	Self-assessment	Peer assessment	Teacher assessment	Average

Teacher comments:

Connections

- Teachers across the grade levels in this program discuss how they can extend or link these lessons to other content areas. Several suggestions follow:

    — Letters can be sent to intended recipients, and the class (for younger and LFS students) or the individual students can record the responses.

    — Students who request information related to a specific content area can share this information with a content-area class.

    — Students may use the information requested to create another product (e.g., brochure, letter, bulletin board, part of a required report).

    — Students may use information requested as a basis for an ongoing project (e.g., information on the number of accidents at a specific corner could lead to a project on teaching students to cross the street more safely).

To document students' progress in reaching the goals set by the various context levels— state, district, program, and classroom—teachers work with students to create writing port- folios across grade levels. In this way, students' progress in attaining these goals can be seen over time and in different classrooms. At the end of each school year, the formative results from assessment are converted to cumulative or summative results. This information, based on the districtwide 5-point writing rubric, is passed on from classrooms to the school and then on to the district. The evidence of student work samples is retained in the students' portfolios.

Goal 3, Standard 2, Grades 9–12

To use English in socially and culturally appropriate ways: Students will use nonverbal communication appropriate to audience, purpose, and setting

Sample Progress Indicators

- compare body language norms among various cultures represented in the classroom or community
- compare gestures and body language acceptable in formal and informal settings
- identify nonverbal cues that cause misunderstanding
- determine the appropriate distance to maintain when standing near someone, depending on the situation
- maintain appropriate level of eye contact with audience while giving an oral presentation
- analyze nonverbal behavior
- describe intent by focusing on a person's nonverbal behavior

Context

Grade Level: Tenth-grade social studies class
English Proficiency Level(s): Intermediate–advanced
Language(s) of Instruction: English
Focus of Instruction: Social studies
Location: Suburban school district in the West

Background

The scenario takes place in a 10th-grade social studies class where half of the students have a native language other than English. Students come from Mexico, China, Palestine, and Russia. Three out of those 10 students have nativelike proficiency in English, whereas the rest are at an intermediate level. The other students are native speakers of English from the mainstream culture. The teacher, Ms. Boland, who has taught ESOL students for 6 years, has taken two graduate-level courses on teaching linguistically and culturally diverse students.

Allocation of Time

The entire sociology unit is approximately 4 weeks in duration. One of the final segments of the unit focuses on nonverbal communication. This segment will last approximately 1 week.

Instructional and Assessment Cycle

PHASE 1: PLANNING

Near the end of a unit on sociology, Ms. Boland plans a segment focusing on nonverbal communication in cross-cultural settings as well as formal and informal settings. Because this is a multicultural class, she will draw from students' personal experiences to enrich class discussions. She decides students will

- view a movie in which the rules of formality are broken (e.g., Marx Brothers films, *My Fair Lady*)

- in heterogeneous groups, list inappropriate behaviors noted in the movie

- participate in a class discussion in which they choose more appropriate behaviors for situations seen in the movie and discuss cultural and situational boundaries for appropriate behavior

- use a Venn diagram[4]

- compare and contrast behaviors in formal and informal settings across cultures

- learn and use related vocabulary

- discuss and record nonverbal communication customs of cultures represented in class

- interview a family member about communication patterns

- present information from the interview to the class

After reviewing her instructional goals and activities, Ms. Boland reflects on how she can monitor the students' progress for this segment of the unit as well as for the remainder of the sociology unit. Figure 2.41 is her outline for integrating assessment into her instructional plan.

PHASE 2: COLLECTING AND RECORDING INFORMATION

While viewing the video, students complete a sheet divided into two sides. One side lists the behaviors and characteristics of the formal situation that they view in the video, and the other side describes the inappropriate and informal behaviors in the video. These sheets are used as the foundation for the smaller group discussions.

Using a group observation sheet (Figure 2.42) Ms. Boland selected when planning the instruction and assessment sequence, she takes notes on how students interact in their groups. She notes the amount of information each student gathered on his or her own

[4] For an example of a Venn diagram, refer to Figure 2.33.

FIGURE 2.41 PURPOSES FOR ASSESSMENT

Students	• Progress toward achieving sample progress indicators: — assess students' class discussion — monitor students' ability to analyze formal and informal situations — monitor students' ability to critically observe nonverbal communication — evaluate students' performance on presentations • Ability to work collaboratively • Ability to interview for specific information
Teacher	• Effectiveness of instructional sequence • Choice of vocabulary words, phrases, or concepts • Determination of need for extension activities
School	• Improvement in communication in school • Improvement in home/school link resulting from interviews

divided sheet during the video viewing. Ms. Boland also notes how often each student participates in the small group and the roles students assume during this participation.

- In groups, students create a Venn diagram to compare behaviors in formal and informal settings from the video. Ms. Boland records the level of interaction and each group's ability to differentiate between formal and informal settings.

- At the end of the classroom discussion that day, Ms. Boland asks students to reflect in their journals on the nonverbal communication customs of their own culture and compare, if possible, with other cultures.

FIGURE 2.42 GROUP OBSERVATION SHEET

Student name:	Individual preparation: (note-taking)	Frequency of participation: (rare, sometimes, often)	Role(s) of student in group:	Lesson focus: (differentiates between formal/ informal behaviors: Y/N)

Individual preparation: In this lesson, individual preparation requires note-taking during the video.

Frequency of participation: Ms. Boland notes if participation is rare, sometimes, or, often.

Role(s) of student in group: This category allows Ms. Boland to note the specifics of how individual students, especially ESOL students, participate. Ms. Boland's notes include verbal and nonverbal participation as well as role-taking, such as facilitator, note-taker, and consensus builder.

Lesson focus: Ms. Boland uses this column to focus on the specific instructional goal of the lesson, which, in this case, is differentiating between formal and informal behaviors.

FIGURE 2.43 PEER CRITIQUE SHEET

Presenter's name _____ Date _____			
	Not at all	**Sometimes**	**All the time**
Makes eye contact with audience.			
Uses appropriate volume.			
Demonstrates clarity of speech.			
Names person interviewed and relationship to presenter.			
Describes two anecdotes demonstrating differences in nonverbal interaction.			

1. Please write two things that you learned from this presentation about nonverbal communication:

2. Please explain one way in which this presenter can improve his or her presentation:

- Following each student's presentation, students critique the presentation using the form shown in Figure 2.43.

Figure 2.44 shows the collection and recording tools for each assessment purpose.

PHASE 3: ANALYZING AND INTERPRETING INFORMATION

As she collects information from this segment of the sociology unit, Ms. Boland evaluates her own instruction and provides feedback to students.

FIGURE 2.44 ALIGNING ASSESSMENT PURPOSE WITH COLLECTING AND RECORDING TOOLS

Purposes	**Collection tools**	**Recording tools**
Assess ability to critically observe nonverbal communication in different settings	Group observation sheet	Grade book
Monitor ability to differentiate between formal and informal settings	Group observation sheet	Grade book
Assess comprehension and retention from classroom discussion	Student journals	Grade book, comments in journal, vocabulary list
Evaluate student performance on presentations	Peer critique sheet and notes	Exchange of peer critique sheets

- To check on students' participation in their cooperative groups, Ms. Boland reviews the group observation sheet. She first analyzes the information to see if there is a correlation between individual preparation and participation in the group discussion. She then compares each student's participation to previous collaborative activities.

- Each group presents the completed Venn diagrams to the class.

- Ms. Boland reviews student journals, writing comments of her own and adding comments from the group observation sheet.

- Students return the completed peer critique sheets to presenters for review.

PHASE 4: REPORTING AND DECISION MAKING

Ms. Boland uses the information she has collected in several ways:

- Ms. Boland allows students to choose their final project for the sociology unit. One of the choices will focus on nonverbal communication. Students will write their own short play in which nonverbal communication is an integral part. Students will be required to submit the play in writing, perform the play in class, and prepare a short discussion about the element of nonverbal communication to follow the performance.

- Ms. Boland shares the findings of the students' interviews and class discussion with other members of her department and her department head. The members of this department and the ESL specialists meet to discuss how to share this information with the students and professional staff of the school in an effort to improve communication in a diverse learning community.

- Because students appeared uncomfortable using the peer critique sheet, Ms. Boland decides that next time she teaches this segment of the unit, she will ask collaborative groups of students to generate their own peer critique sheet template. Groups will share their results, and a final critique sheet will be developed.

Discussion and Reflection

This lesson takes place in a diverse, mainstream classroom. Although the curriculum is not sheltered, Ms. Boland makes accommodations for the ESOL students by using mixed ability groups, multimedia, graphic organizers, and targeted vocabulary learning. An after-school tutor provides additional support for these language learners.

Notice that, in this lesson, Ms. Boland does not collect the Venn diagrams. However, in an earlier lesson in this unit, when she was teaching students how to create Venn diagrams, the students' completed products were reviewed as evidence of learning.

Ms. Boland uses different assessment strategies, which allow students to demonstrate what they know in different ways (i.e., journal, group discussion, interview, presentation). There is a combination of teacher-driven assessments and peer assessments. Peer assessments allow students to take more responsibility in the classroom and encourage self-assessment. If the students feel that the critique sheet is valuable, they could adapt it to use as a self-assessment tool in presentations they make for other classes.

Cross-cultural communication is integrated into both instruction and assessment through family member interviews, presentations, and journal entries. This emphasizes the importance of linking individual cultural norms to the classroom.

Connections

- Ms. Boland knows that the district is planning a staff development day focused on cross-cultural communication. After talking with the district person in charge of this event, she invites several of her students to form a panel to present some of the information they have collected and prepared for this lesson.

- Ms. Boland has created the peer critique sheet illustrated in this lesson. In earlier lessons in this unit, however, the students developed a peer critique sheet that focused on key aspects of the language to be learned.

Goal 3, Standard 3, Grades 4–8

To use English in socially and culturally appropriate ways: Students will use appropriate learning strategies to extend their communicative competence

Sample Progress Indicators

- evaluate behaviors in different situations
- model behavior and language use of others in different situations and settings
- observe language use and behaviors of peers in different settings
- rehearse different ways of speaking according to the formality of the setting

Context

Grade Level: Eighth-grade bilingual class
English Proficiency Level(s):   Intermediate
Language(s) of Instruction: Khmer and English
Focus of Instruction: Community service
Location: Urban school district in the Northeast

Background

Mr. Seng's eighth-grade class of 12 Cambodian students is in its third year of a transitional bilingual education program and will make the transition out of the bilingual program next year when the students enter high school. It is now March, and Mr. Seng has been working with this class for much of the academic year. Although he has observed the development of the students' command of a range of language structures, he knows that they need to develop their use of English in socially and culturally appropriate ways. He also recognizes the fact that these students need to continue to develop their repertoire of learning strategies so that they can function as self-learners. All middle school students in the district are expected to perform 10 hours of community service as part of the social studies curriculum. Mr. Seng views the community service requirement as an ideal approach for helping his students practice English in a meaningful way and take on a greater responsibility for managing their learning experiences.

Allocation of Time

Mr. Seng has arranged for the students to visit a nearby nursing home for 2 hours after school, 1 day a week for 5 weeks. Mr. Seng has designed a 2-week unit to prepare students for their first visit to the nursing home.

Instructional and Assessment Cycle

PHASE 1: PLANNING

Mr. Seng has planned a series of activities as part of this unit. The week before the first visit to the nursing home, the director of the nursing home will come to class and speak to the students about the patients. The patients at the nursing home are mostly Polish Americans and Greek Americans who have lived in the city for most of their lives.

Next, Mr. Seng will show a clip from a television movie that has scenes in a nursing home. He will direct students to pay attention to the way the nurses and the family members speak to the patients during the clip. After viewing the film, the students will discuss as a class the way people speak to each other. Asking students to draw on their developing awareness of language variation, Mr. Seng will lead a discussion about how students might address their particular patient.

Mr. Seng will then replay 4 minutes from the clip and ask students to write down one or two sentences from the dialogue. Selected students will write their sentences on the board for class review. Mr. Seng will replay the full clip one last time so that students can take notes on the physical movements of the people who interact with the patients and then discuss what they have seen.

As a final activity, students will role-play several situations using the fish bowl technique. In this technique, students sit on chairs that are placed in a circle. Three students take turns entering the circle to play a patient, nurse, and student visitor. Mr. Seng describes scenarios, such as the first time the student and the patient meet, a visit on the patient's birthday, a misunderstanding about patting one's head or arm on occasion, a visit when the patient must receive some medication, and the last visit scheduled for the class. Students practice what they will say, and classmates give suggestions to improve the conversations.

The following chart (Figure 2.45) shows how these activities are related to targeted learning strategy goals:

PHASE 2: COLLECTING AND RECORDING INFORMATION

So that students can monitor their progress in working toward targeted SPIs, they engage in several assessment activities throughout the series of planned instructional activities.

Student Logs

To help them reflect more systematically on how language varies, students keep a log of language use within specific social situations. Students enter language observations at various points throughout this unit.

FIGURE 2.45 ALIGNING SAMPLE PROGRESS INDICATORS AND INSTRUCTIONAL ACTIVITIES

Sample progress indicators	Instructional activity
Evaluate behaviors in different situations	• Show and discuss video clip showing varied language use. • Students role-play several situations, varying their roles and situations.
Model behavior and language use of others in different situations and settings	• Show and discuss video clip showing varied language use. • Students discuss how they may use this information with their own patient.
Observe language use and behaviors of peers in different settings	• Show and discuss video clip showing varied language use. • Students role-play several situations, varying their roles and situations.
Rehearse different ways of speaking according to the formality of the setting	• Students role-play several situations, varying their roles and situations.

- From time to time during the nursing home director's visit, Mr. Seng interprets medical or other unfamiliar terminology in Khmer or asks one of the students to do so, thereby ensuring all students understand the information. Students enter unfamiliar terms into their logs to create dictionaries for this activity.

- Students use the logs to record their sentences from the video clip Mr. Seng shows.

- Students also record notes on the physical movements of the people who interact with patients in the video.

Video Note Sheet

Mr. Seng provides students with a collecting tool to help them as they note the ways in which nurses and family members speak to the patients in the video clip (see Figure 2.46).

Fishbowl Peer Critique Checklist

To help students critique one another's performances as they role-play different scenarios in the fish bowl, Mr. Seng provides the following checklist (Figure 2.47). Students rate each performer (+/−) and note suggestions for improvement in the end column.

PHASE 3: ANALYZING AND INTERPRETING INFORMATION

The kind of data collected throughout this scenario helps Mr. Seng and his students monitor the development of the important language learning strategies targeted in this scenario. For the most part, the analyses consist of reviewing data collected to determine patterns of language use.

- Mr. Seng and individual students review the student logs and video note sheets, adding comments if appropriate.

FIGURE 2.46 VIDEO NOTE SHEET

Form of address used (Title)	Character in the video who uses this language form	Why do you think this language form is used?
Grandma	granddaughter	Family members use informal forms of address to show personal relationships.
Mrs. Kish	nurse	Staff at the nursing home show respect toward patients by using a formal form of address.

- Fishbowl Peer Critique Checklist provides an opportunity for peers as well as Mr. Seng to evaluate other students' performances in a variety of situations. When inappropriate use is identified, Mr. Seng and other students provide feedback and suggestions for improvement.

PHASE 4: REPORTING AND DECISION MAKING

Mr. Seng's students receive feedback directly from Mr. Seng and their fellow classmates either in the form of comments during class discussions or on the written forms developed to accompany the tasks in this unit. Students also review their own logs, note sheets, and checklists to reflect on their use of learning strategies. Students assume the responsibility for keeping and using the feedback provided by Mr. Seng and other students. Note that the results of these assessments are unlikely to be used in high-stakes decision making about these students' academic careers, although supporting their development of learning strategies may be crucial to their academic success. Often, information about learning strategies is used in a formative way to monitor student progress.

FIGURE 2.47 FISHBOWL PEER CRITIQUE CHECKLIST

Scenarios	Patient	Nurse	Student visitor	Suggestions
1. First visit				
2. Birthday visit				
3. Misunderstanding				
4. Medication visit				
5. Last visit				

Discussion and Reflection

Learning strategies are often described as important components of language learning, yet assessing them is often difficult. In this scenario, the assessment activities function as opportunities for students to reflect on the development of those learning strategies. Thus, the teacher's role is less central throughout the instructional and assessment cycle. Students are expected to take active roles as they engage in both the instructional activities as well as the assessment ones. This active role is crucial if students are to develop learning strategies that extend their communicative competence.

The students in this scenario are in middle school. As students mature, it becomes even more appropriate for them to take responsibility for their own learning. Thus, this scenario has emphasized the students' role in monitoring the development of learning strategies.

Connections

- Some scenarios have demonstrated connections between students' community and classroom activities. In this scenario, students perform community service by visiting nursing home residents. Their community service project allows the students to observe and comment on cultural norms of treatment of the elderly in the United States. In addition, students can apply learning strategies to help them better identify cultural norms. In many cultures, intergenerational ties are a part of daily life. Therefore, opportunities like this allow students opportunities to build on their own cultural competence. This scenario shows that ESOL students, like their monolingual English-speaking peers, can contribute to the community and learn from their volunteer experiences.

- It may be interesting to compare this scenario on learning strategies to the one for Goal 1, Standard 3, another scenario focused on learning strategies. In that scenario, the teacher and students assess strategy use in a variety of ways appropriate to the setting. Both scenarios provide important information on assessment of strategies.

A *Plan for* Standards-Based *Instruction and* Assessment

We have provided the following checklist (Figure 2.48) as a guide for the systematic implementation of a standards-based approach to instruction and assessment. The activities reprise the steps teachers take in the scenarios; the date column sets the stage for creating a time line. This tool should help in designing your own assessment process.

FIGURE 2.48 STANDARDS-BASED INSTRUCTION AND ASSESSMENT CHECKLIST

Activity	Date
1. Select a standard, theme, issue, or problem for instruction with students.	
2. Decide on the content and language areas for instruction and assessment.	
3. Select ESL and content standard(s) to be addressed.	
4. Identify core ideas and concepts for the lesson(s) or unit.	
5. Brainstorm ways that students will use higher level thinking skills.	
6. Determine the necessary resources for the instructional activity and assessment.	
7. Determine the processes for and products of the instructional activity and assessment.	
8. Design a final project (e.g., part of a portfolio, essay, demonstration) for the final assessment piece. Students should have two or three choices.	
9. Collaborate with other teachers to select appropriate rubrics to assess the project.	
10. Design instructional activities and assessments that feed into the final product (e.g., small essays, class discussions, journal entries). Work with the class to create a time line for project completion.	
11. Identify appropriate rubrics and observation checklists used for the teacher's assessment, student self-assessment, and peer assessment. Share rubrics with students.	
12. Match student products to the criteria of the rubric. Select appropriate samples to serve as examples of each level of performance for current and future use to benchmark.	
13. Work with other teachers to reach consensus on student performance using the rubrics and student samples.	
14. If using portfolios, design a summary sheet to chart students' overall performances.	
15. Work with school and district administrators to coordinate portfolio efforts within and across grades.	
16. Incorporate curricular/instructional/assessment topics into the school's professional development activities.	

Part 3:
Understanding
and Using
Assessment Data

Understanding and Using Assessment Data

Selecting Types of Data for Assessment

FORMATIVE VERSUS SUMMATIVE INFORMATION

Assessment information can be classified as either *formative* or *summative*. Formative information is collected on an ongoing basis to help make day-to-day decisions about students and instruction. This information is specific to the lesson being taught and, in the case of the scenarios, reflective of the SPIs being addressed. Other information from assessment is considered summative. It is systematically collected on a specified schedule, such as on an annual basis. Summative data are used for programmatic decision making, such as determining eligibility for services and monitoring student progress over time. End-of-term grades are also considered summative.

The scenarios, in large part, provide formative feedback to teachers and students. The kinds of information gained from assessment vary tremendously from student to student and from classroom to classroom. Reliability or consistency of results is most important in summative assessment because results may carry high stakes for students, such as fulfilling graduation requirements.

Formative assessment folds into summative assessment. Information gathered on a short-term basis assists in long-term decision making. In the scenarios, different tools are used for collecting information about student classroom performance over time. We assume that formative assessment of individual SPIs leads to summative assessment of standards. In addition, at the summative level, information may be provided by standardized, commercially developed, norm-referenced tests.

STANDARDIZED TESTING

Commercially developed, norm-referenced tests may be a part of school life. However, they have intentionally been excluded from the scenarios. There are several reasons for this decision:

1. Teachers have little to no control over their administration.

2. The scenarios focus, in large part, on formative, not summative assessment.

3. We feel it is not appropriate to mention some tests to the exclusion of others. There are several resources on the Internet that may be helpful in finding information on standardized tests; each resource also offers links to other related sites.

   - *Buros Institute of Mental Measurement* (http://www.unl.edu/buros) includes summary and technical information on tests in *Tests in Print* as well as a test locator and articles on fair testing practice.

   - *ERIC Clearinghouse on Assessment and Evaluation* (http://www.ericae.net) has a wide range of links and topics including alternate assessment/performance-based assessment, computer-assisted testing, disabilities and their implications for assessment, early childhood assessment, elementary and secondary education, fairness in testing, and goals and standards. In addition to articles on assessment, there are links to a number of electronic discussion lists for K–12 educators.

Blueprints and Time Lines for Assessment

Ideally, teachers should develop a blueprint or framework for designing summative assessment. A blueprint helps guide the development of a single instrument or organize multiple collection tools. It is also helpful in helping teachers assign the relative weight of SPIs, standards, and goals. The blueprint, by providing the specifications for determining the attainment of ESL standards, makes it easier for teachers to manage data in the long run.

Figure 3.1 shows how a blueprint may be configured using different types of documentation to measure student attainment of the ESL goals and standards. First, the ways of documenting assessment, as depicted in the scenarios, are identified for each standard and goal. Then, taking Goal 2, Standard 2, as an example, the percent that each assessment contributes to the total measurement of the standard is noted in its respective cell.

It is relatively easy to develop time lines from a blueprint of the overall assessment process as applied to all ESL goals and standards and to show how the blueprint correlates

FIGURE 3.1 BLUEPRINT FOR ASSESSMENT OF ESOL STUDENTS

	Checklists	Rating scales	Holistic scales	Other data sources	Standardized tests*	Total
Goal 1, Standard 1				X		
Goal 1, Standard 2	X					
Goal 1, Standard 3						
Goal 2, Standard 1						
Goal 2, Standard 2	X 15%	X 15%	X 15%	X 5%	X 50%	100%
Goal 2, Standard 3				X		
Goal 3, Standard 1		X				
Goal 3, Standard 2				X		
Goal 3, Standard 3						

Note. *In this table and the one that follows, we use the term *standardized tests* because it is the more commonly used term. However, the more descriptive term would be *commercially available, nationally norm-referenced tests.*

with the program of instruction. Individual cells of the matrix may be color coded, for example, to correspond to the season (or month) of data collection. The development of time lines should be incorporated into the planning phase of assessment.

Sometimes educators prefer to create a month-by-month time line for data collection. Figure 3.2 identifies five data sources that could be used throughout the school year on a monthly basis. Each X marks the time frame for systematic gathering of data for the specified source.

Another way to create a time line for data collection is illustrated in Figure 2.9 for Goal 1, Standard 2, for Grades Pre-K–3. In this scenario, the teacher manages the data on students for a specific standard by establishing a weekly and monthly schedule. Four groups of students rotate activities over the month so that the teacher can focus on assessing a small number of students at one time.

A tremendous amount of performance data is generated by students everyday inside and outside their classrooms. Teachers need to have a working knowledge of which kinds of information are important to document as part of formative classroom assessment. In addition, teachers need to be aware of the kinds of formative information that contribute to summative assessment information and, ultimately, the measurement of the attainment of the ESL standards.

Setting Performance Levels for ESOL Students

Phase 3 of the assessment process focuses on analyzing and interpreting the information we have collected and recorded. To determine the extent to which ESOL students have attained the ESL standards, we need to define performance standards and set performance levels.

FIGURE 3.2 TIME LINE FOR COLLECTION OF STUDENT DATA FOR ESL TEACHERS

	Oral language observation	Informal reading inventory	Student journal writing	Content-area projects	Standardized tests
August	X	X	X		
September			X	X	
October			X		
November	X		X	X	
December			X		
January		X	X	X	
February			X		
March	X		X	X	
April			X		X
May			X	X	
June	X		X		

Because the scenarios present performance-based activities and tasks, rubrics are the best way to document what ESOL students do.

THE ROLE OF RUBRICS IN DOCUMENTING PERFORMANCE

The use of a documentation form or scoring rubric with carefully defined criteria connected to the ESL standards sets clear expectations for students and assists teachers in reaching consensus in analyzing and interpreting assessment information. SPIs from the ESL standards may serve as the criteria against which student work is measured. In addition to serving as a yardstick for measuring student performance, rubrics often serve as the mechanism for translating standards into practice and attaching meaning to what students do.

STEPS IN SETTING PERFORMANCE LEVELS

Within the scenarios, we have introduced an array of rubrics that may be used by teachers and students. To determine the movement or progress of ESOL students toward a standard, teachers and administrators must think about how assessment information is to be analyzed and reported. Several questions come to mind when setting performance levels:

Which types of rubrics or documentation forms are being used to interpret student performance?

Setting the performance level of standard attainment for a checklist, for example, is different from setting the performance level of a holistic scale or anecdotal notes. For a checklist, an ESOL student may demonstrate acceptable performance when 80% of the items or SPIs have been marked. For a holistic rubric, an ESOL student's work may correspond to scoring criteria at Level 3 of a 4-point scale. This example may be found in the scenario for Goal 2, Standard 2, Grades 9–12. For anecdotal notes taken by a teacher, the presence of a certain number of prespecified behaviors may indicate standards attainment.

How many approaches to assessment are necessary in determining performance levels?

There are multiple approaches to assessment, such as performance-based assessment, criterion-referenced assessment, and commercially developed, norm-referenced assessment. Each approach yields different kinds of information. Ideally, more than one approach or data source should be used in making decisions regarding attainment of standards. If there are established performance levels, and assessment information is plotted on to a form that identifies each approach, a student profile on progress toward meeting the ESL standards can be produced.

How are performance levels going to be set and how many performance levels should be set?

Often, states use grade levels as benchmarks. In *ESL Standards for Pre-K–12 Students* (TESOL, 1997), however, the goals and standards are presented by grade-level clusters: pre-K–3, 4–8, and 9–12. It might be appropriate to use language proficiency as a benchmark of perform-ance. *ESL Standards* use limited formal schooling, beginning, intermediate, and advanced designations. Therefore, setting performance levels according to language proficiency designations requires benchmarking at several places (e.g., the point at which a beginning ESOL student is distinguished from an intermediate student and the point at which an intermediate student is distinguished from an advanced student).

Where are performance levels set?

The placement of performance levels depends on the type of rubric or documentation form that is used in interpreting the assessment information. If, as in the previous example, a 4-point holistic scale is part of performance assessment, the benchmark needs to be set so there is room for students to exceed (at a level above the benchmark) as well as to fall below the benchmarked level.

How many pieces of evidence are necessary before you are confident that an ESOL student has attained the standards?

This question is quite tricky, because states generally rely only on their state assessment to make high-stakes decisions. It is best, however, to have at least two pieces of evidence from two different assessment approaches to confirm that the designated standard has been addressed on more than one occasion and that the ESOL student has demonstrated proficiency at the stated performance or benchmark level.

What types of work samples and other student data are going to be used to validate the assignment of a performance level?

ESL and classroom teachers should collaborate in selecting student work that best illustrates the criteria specified in a rubric for each performance level (i.e., if using a 4-point scale, agreed-upon samples of student work that match the criteria at all four levels are necessary).

STEPS IN DETERMINING INTERRATER AGREEMENT AMONG TEACHERS

In traditional norm-referenced assessment, consistency or reliability is internal to the measure itself. In performance assessment, reliability is linked to interrater agreement among raters. This means that the raters scoring student work, usually teachers, need to agree on the score. Rubrics help establish a basis for reliability (a necessary technical quality of assessment) by offering a uniform set of criteria against which teachers make judgments based on student work.

Teachers need to reach consensus in regard to scoring at each performance level of a rubric. Work samples, taken from the entire range of ESOL student performance, serve as models or anchors for scoring other student products. ESL, bilingual, and classroom teachers who work with ESOL students should spend time to establish interrater agreement for performance assessment as part of their school's ongoing professional development. Here are some steps teachers may follow:

- Determine the percent of agreement to reach among yourselves. Generally, 85% or above is acceptable and considered reliable.

- Identify the scale or rubric (in this case, we will refer to the 4-point holistic scale) to be used and collect student samples.

- Become familiar with the criteria of the rubric by pointing out examples from student work. Student work used for anchors should represent the midrange within a performance level. In a 4-point scale, for example, there is room for 25% variation.

- Select a partner and 10 student work samples. Set up a rater sheet like the one in Figure 3.3.

- Use the criteria on the scoring rubric, and individually score each of the 10 student work samples. On the sheet, write the numeral that corresponds to the point on the scale that best describes the student's performance.

- Working in pairs, mark the scores that do not match in the third column. Put an *a–* to indicate one level lower or *a+* to indicate one level higher than Rater B's scores.

- Determine the number of scores that match. Because there are 10 samples, it is easy to convert the total score into a percent correct. This is your interrater agreement.

- Discuss your discrepant ratings with your partner. Defend your score based on the rubric's criteria.

- Reach 100% consensus or agreement and try again on another set of student work samples.

Discussion

This activity yields two important results. By reaching agreement, teachers increase the reliability of the assessment. The activity itself—teachers talking about instructional goals and assessment of students in attaining these goals—is in itself a rich professional development experience.

FIGURE 3.3 INTERRATER AGREEMENT SCORING SHEET

	Rater A	Rater B	Amount of discrepancy (+/-)
Work sample 1			
Work sample 2			
Work sample 3			
Work sample 4			
Work sample 5			

Assessment Forms Used in the Scenarios

Figure	Name	Page	Grade Level(s)
2.5	Self-Assessment for Group Participation	31	4
2.6	Preposition Tally Sheet	31	4
2.7	Continuation of Preposition Tally Sheet	32	4
2.8	Student Information Sheet	34	4
2.9	Plan for Collecting Data	37	2
2.10	Book Talk Checklist	38	2
2.13	Learning Strategies Checklist	44	7
2.14	Science Log	50	8
2.15	Graphic Organizer for the Scientific Method	50	8
2.16	Learning Strategies Inventory	51	8
2.17	Oral Interaction Checklist	51	8
2.18	Science Grade Report Sheet	52	8
2.20	Task-Specific Rating Scale	57	1
2.21	Family Member Checklist	58	1
2.22	District Summary Checklist	59	1
2.24	Observation Guide for Conducting Science Activities	66	4/5
2.26	Debate Information and Sources Inventory	71	11
2.27	Debate Sources Checklist	72	11
2.28	Debate Team Checklist	73	11
2.29	Departmental Writing Rubric	74	11
2.30	Graphic Organizer A	79	11
2.31	Graphic Organizer B	79	11
2.32	Graphic Organizer C	80	11
2.33	Graphic Organizer D	81	11
2.35	Learning Log/Self-Assessment Form	87	9–11
2.36	Teacher Observation Note Sheet	88	9–11
2.39	Six-Trait Rating Scale	97	4–12
2.40	Rating Sheet for Oral or Written Assessment	98	4–12
2.42	Group Observation Sheet	102	10
2.43	Peer Critique Sheet	103	10
2.46	Video Note Sheet	109	8
2.47	Fishbowl Peer Critique Checklist	109	8
2.48	Standard-Based Instruction and Assessment Checklist	111	K–12
3.1	Blueprint for Assessment of ESOL Students	116	K–12
3.2	Time Line for Collection of Student Data for ESL Teachers	117	K–12
3.3	Interrater Agreement Scoring Sheet	120	K–12

Glossary

academic language: language used in the learning of academic subject matter in formal schooling contexts; aspects of language strongly associated with literacy and academic achievement, including specific academic terms or technical language, and speech registers related to each field of study

additive bilingualism: a process by which individuals develop proficiency in a second language subsequent to or simultaneous with the development of proficiency in the primary language, without loss of the primary language; a bilingual situation where the addition of a second language and culture are unlikely to replace or displace the first language and culture

aggregated data: all data from a commercially available, norm-referenced test not segregated by gender, language background, ethnicity, or other categories

alignment: the match among the ESL standards, curriculum, instruction, and assessment

alternative assessment: the systematic collection, analysis, and reporting of student performance or achievement information from sources other than a standardized, norm-referenced test

assessment: systematic cycle of planning, collecting, analyzing, interpreting, and reporting information on student performance, preferably based on different sources over time

assessment standards: statements that establish guidelines for evaluating student performance and attainment of content standards; often include philosophical statements of good assessment practice (see performance standards)

biculturalism: near nativelike knowledge of two cultures; includes the ability to respond effectively to the different demands of these two cultures

bilingual instruction: provision of instruction in school settings through the medium of two languages, usually a native and a second language; the proportion of the instructional day delivered in each language varies by the type of the bilingual education program in which instruction is offered and the goals of said program

checklist: a form to document student performance on assessment tasks to indicate whether a competency/skill has been attained or not (also called a dichotomous scale)

communicative competence: the ability to recognize and produce authentic and appropriate language correctly and fluently in any situation; use of language in realistic, everyday settings; involves grammatical competence, sociolinguistic competence, discourse competence, and strategic competence

content-based ESL: a model of language education that integrates language and content instruction in the second language classroom; a second language learning approach where second language teachers use instructional materials, learning tasks, and classroom techniques from academic content areas as the vehicle for developing second language, content, cognitive, and study skills

content standards: statements that define what one is expected to know and be able to do in a content area; the knowledge, skills, processes, and other understandings that schools should teach in order for students to attain high levels of competency in challenging subject matter; the subject-specific knowledge, processes, and skills that schools are expected to teach and students are expected to learn

criterion-referenced assessment: assessment that is based on preestablished criteria or descriptions of language ability rather than on performances of other students

cross-cultural competence: ability to function according to the cultural rules of more than one cultural system; ability to respond in culturally sensitive and appropriate ways according to the cultural demands of a given situation

culture: the sum total of the ways of life of a people; includes norms, learned behavior patterns, attitudes, and artifacts; also involves traditions, habits, or customs; how people behave, feel, and interact; the means by which they order and interpret the world; ways of perceiving, relating, and interpreting events based on established social norms; a system of standards for perceiving, believing, evaluating, and acting

descriptors: broad categories of discrete, representative behaviors that students exhibit when they meet a standard

dialect: a regional variety of language distinguished by features of vocabulary, grammar, and pronunciation that differ from other regional varieties

disaggregated data: test data that reflect separate groups of test scores by specific categories such as language background, ethnicity, or gender

discrete-point tests: a test that examines skills in isolation

ESL: the field of English as a second language; courses, classes, and programs designed for students learning English as an additional language

ESOL students: English speakers of other languages; refers to learners who are identified as still in the process of acquiring English as an additional language; students who may not speak English at all or, at least, do not speak, understand, and write English with the same facility as their classmates because they did not grow up speaking English but primarily spoke another language at home

evaluation: interpretation of assessment data that have been scored and analyzed to make judgments or draw inferences about the quality or worth of student work and educational programs

formative evaluation: ongoing collection, analysis, reporting of data about student performance in order to guide instruction and learning

genre: a category of literary composition characterized by a particular style, form, or content; a historical novel is one fictional genre

holistic score: a single, integrated score or level on a rubric, with specified criteria, based on a student's performance

home language: language(s) spoken in the student's home by significant others (e.g., family members, caregivers) who reside there; sometimes used as a synonym for first language (L1), primary language, or native language

journal: a written record of thoughts, opinions, and reactions recorded on a regular basis; an alternative assessment technique that asks students to respond to prompts to determine content knowledge

interrater reliability: a technical measure of the degree of agreement between two raters rating the same assessment item (e.g., student writing sample) using the same scale

language minority: a student who comes from a home in which a language other than English is primarily spoken; the student may or may not speak English well

language proficiency: the level of competence at which an individual is able to use language for basic communicative tasks as well as academic purposes

language variety: variations of a language used by particular groups of people; includes regional dialects characterized by distinct vocabularies, speech patterns, and grammatical features; may also vary by social group (sociolect) or idiosyncratically for a particular individual (idiolect)

large-scale assessment: district- or statewide assessment programs that include all or most students; often used as accountability tool to measure how well the system is doing its job of educating all students

learning strategies: mental activities or actions that assist in enhancing learning outcomes; may include metacognitive strategies (e.g., planning for learning, monitoring one's own comprehension and production, evaluating one's performance), cognitive strategies (e.g., mental or physical manipulation of the material) or social/affective strategies (e.g., interacting with another person to assist learning, using self-talk to persist at a difficult task until resolution)

linguistic competence: a broad term used to describe the totality of a given individual's language ability; the underlying language system believed to exist as inferred from an individual's language performance

L1: primary or first language spoken by an individual

matrix: a type of rubric that has separate cells with specified criteria created by crossing the assessment category with the levels of attainment

multilingualism: ability to speak more than two languages; proficiency in many languages

multiple measures: a variety of assessment types to determine student performance; often used to make educational decisions so as not to rely on a single assessment

native language: primary or first language (L1) spoken by an individual

nonverbal communication: paralinguistic and nonlinguistic messages that can be transmitted in conjunction with language or without the aid of language; paralinguistic mechanisms include intonation, stress, rate of speech, and pauses or hesitations; nonlinguistic behaviors include gestures, facial expressions, and body language, among others

norm-referenced assessment: an assessment whose scores are based on relative performances of other students performing the same task

performance-based assessment: tasks that require students to construct a response, create a product, or demonstrate applications of knowledge that are interpreted using preestablished criteria.

performance standards: statements that refer to how well students are meeting a content standard; they specify the quality and effect of student performance at various levels of competency (benchmarks) in the subject matter; these standards specify how students must demonstrate their knowledge and skills and can show student progress toward meeting a content standard

portfolio assessment: a systematic collection of the processes and products of a student's original work along with associated documentation that has been determined, in part, by student choice based on a set of defined targets with clear-cut criteria and a specified purpose

primary language: first or native language spoken by an individual

proficiency-based assessment: an assessment based on a person's holistic language proficiency

progress indicators: assessable, observable activities that students may perform to show progress toward meeting the standard; these activities are organized by grade-level clusters

proxemics: the study of distances maintained by speakers of different languages as they speak to each other or others

proximity norms: cultural behaviors associated with the distance and body positioning maintained by members of the same culture during conversation

pullout instruction: in the case of ESL pullout instruction, students are withdrawn from their regular classrooms for one or more periods a week for special classes of ESL instruction in small groups

rating scale: a form for documenting student performance on assessment tasks that indicates the range (e.g., low to high) on which a competency/skill has been attained (also called a Likert scale)

realia: concrete objects used to relate classroom teaching to real life (e.g., use of actual foods and supermarket circulars to develop the language related to foods and food purchasing)

register: usage of different varieties of language (depending on the setting), the relationship among the individuals involved in the communication, and the function of the interaction; a register is a form of a language that is appropriate to the social or functional context

regular class: (as used in this book and ESL Standards for Pre-K–12 Students [TESOL, 1997]) refers to a class with or without ESOL students that does not systematically accommodate the language learning needs of ESOL students; may be a regular elementary class or a subject-area class at a secondary level where all instruction is delivered and materials are provided almost exclusively in English; sometimes referred to as a mainstream class

reliability: a technical measure to determine an assessment's ability to produce consistent, accurate results

rubric: a scale with descriptive criteria at each score point or level; used to document student performance

scenario: a hypothetical instructional or assessment situation

self-assessment: a student's reflection and analysis of his or her own work, including the processes and strategies used in creating the product, either at one point in time or over time

self-contained ESL class: an ESL class with only ESOL students; instruction may focus on ESL or content or both for one or more periods of the day; no pullout instruction is used

sheltered instruction: an approach in which students develop knowledge in specific subject areas through the medium of English, their second language; teachers adjust the language demands of the lesson in many ways, such as modifying speech rate and tone, using context clues and models extensively, relating instruction to student experience, adapting the language of texts or tasks, and using certain methods familiar to language teachers (e.g., demonstrations, visuals, graphic organizers, cooperative work) to make academic instruction more accessible to students developing proficiency in English

social functions: use of language to accomplish various purposes, such as asking for or giving information, describing past actions, expressing feelings, and expressing regret

social language: the aspects of language proficiency strongly associated with basic fluency in face-to-face-interaction; natural speech in social interactions, including those that occur in a classroom

sociocultural competence: ability to function effectively in a particular social or cultural context according to the rules or expectancies for behavior held by members of that social or cultural group

sociolinguistic competence: related to communicative competence; the extent to which language is appropriately understood and used in a given situation (e.g., the ability to make apologies, give compliments, and politely refuse requests)

stakeholder: those who are involved in the assessment process and concerned about assessment results, such as students, parents, teachers, and the community

standards-based assessment: the systematic planning, gathering, analyzing, and reporting of student performance according to the ESL standards

subtractive bilingualism: the learning of a majority language at the expense of the first; refers to cases where the first language and culture have low status and where, because of this, learners are encouraged to divest themselves of their first language and culture and to replace them with the second language and culture; primary language attrition or loss and cultural anomie (e.g., uncertainty, alienation) are often the result of a subtractive bilingual situation

summative evaluation: the collection, analysis, and reporting of information at the culmination of a marking period, semester, academic year, or other set time frame

task: an instructional or assessment activity that invites a varied response to a question, issue, or problem

test: a sample of student behavior at one point in time

two-way bilingual immersion program: a program in which monolingual English-speaking children study the regular school curriculum alongside children who are native speakers of the target, or second, language; a portion of the instructional day is taught in English, and another portion is in the target language; such programs aim for additive bilingualism and biculturalism for all the students involved

validity: a technical measure of an assessment's match between the information collected by the items and its specified purposes

vernacular: language or dialect native to a region or country; normal spoken form of a language; includes nonstandard dialects

vignette: a description of an instructional sequence drawn from the real-life experiences of teachers

References and Resources

American Educational Research Association, American Psychological Association, & National Council on Measurement in Education. (1985). *Standards for educational and psychological testing.* Washington, DC: American Psychological Association.

Anstrom, K. (1997). *Academic achievement for secondary language minority students: Standards, measures and promising practices.* Washington, DC: National Clearinghouse for Bilingual Education. Retrieved November 4, 2000, from the World Wide Web: http://www.ncbe.gwu.edu/ncbepubs /reports/acadach.html.

Association for Supervision and Curriculum Development.(1991). *Expanding student assessment.* Alexandria, VA: Author.

Association for Supervision and Curriculum Development. (1996). *A teacher's guide to performance-based learning and assessment.* Alexandria, VA: Author.

Arter, J. (1996). *Assessing student performance: An ASCD professional inquiry kit.* Alexandria, VA: Association for Supervision and Curriculum Development.

Bouffler, C. (Ed.). (1993). *Literacy evaluation: Issues & practicalities.* Portsmouth, NH: Heinemann.

Brown, J. D., & Hudson, T. (1998). The alternatives in language assessment. *TESOL Journal , 32*(4), 653–675.

Burger, D. (1997). *Designing a sustainable standards-based assessment system.* Retrieved January 4, 2001, from the World Wide Web: http://www.mcrel.org/products/standards/designing.asp.

Burke, K. (Ed.). (1992). *Authentic assessment: A collection.* Palatine, IL: Skylight.

Burke, K. (1994). *The mindful school: How to assess authentic learning.* Palatine, IL: Skylight

Daly, E. (Ed.). (1991). *Monitoring children's language development: Holistic assessment in the classroom.* Portsmouth, NH: Heinemann.

Darling-Hammond, L. (1994). Performance-based assessment and educational equity. *Harvard Educational Review, 64*(1), 5–30.

Darling-Hammond, L., Ancess, J., & Falk, B. (1995). *Authentic assessment in action: Studies of schools and students at work.* New York: National Center for Restructuring Education, Schools, and Teaching, Teachers College, Columbia University.

Easton, J., & Perlman, C. (1994). *The CPS performance assessment idea book.* Chicago: Board of Education of the City of Chicago.

Evaluation Assistance Center-East. (1996). *Promoting excellence: Ensuring academic success for limited English proficient students.* Washington, DC: George Washington University.

Farr, B. P., & Trumbell, E. (1997). *Assessment alternatives for diverse classrooms.* Norwood, MA: Christopher-Gordon.

Foreign language assessment in the elementary school. (1991–1992, Winter). *FLES News, 5,* p. 3.

Fradd, S. H., & McGee, P. L. (1994). *Instructional assessment: An integrative approach to evaluating student performance.* Reading, MA: Addison-Wesley.

Genesee, F., & Upshur, J. A. (1996). *Classroom-based evaluation in second language education.* New York: Cambridge University Press.

Glatthorn, A. A. (1998). *Performance assessment and standards-based curricula: The achievement cycle.* Larchmont, NY: Eye on Education.

Glazer, S. M. (1998). *Assessment is instruction: Reading, writing, spelling, and phonics for all learners.* Norwood, MA: Christopher-Gordon.

Gottlieb, M. (1997). A peek into portfolio practices. In A. Huhta, V. Kohonen, L. Kurki-Suonio, & S. Luoma (Eds.), *Current developments and alternatives in language assessment: Proceedings of LTRC 96* (pp. 23–36). Jyvaskyla, Finland: University of Jyvaskyla.

Gottlieb, M. (1999). Assessing ESOL adolescents: Balancing accessibility to learn with accountability for learning. In C. J. Faltis & P. Wolfe (Eds.), *So much to say: Teenagers, bilingualism and ESL at the secondary school* (pp. 176–201). New York: Teachers College Press.

Gottlieb, M. (1999). *The language proficiency handbook: A practitioner's guide to instructional assessment.* Springfield: Illinois State Board of Education.

Gottlieb, M. (in press). Promising assessment practices for language minority students: National, state, and school perspectives. In M. del Rosario Basterra (Ed.), *Excellence and equity for language minority students: Critical issues and promising practices.* Chevy Chase, MD: The Mid-Atlantic Equity Consortium.

Guskey, T. R. (Ed.). (1994). *High stakes performance assessment: Perspectives on Kentucky's educational reform.* Thousand Oaks, CA: Corwin.

Harp, B. (1996). *A handbook of literacy assessment and evaluation.* Norwood, MA: Christopher-Gordon.

Hein, G. E., & Price, S. (1994). *Active assessment for active science.* Portsmouth, NH: Heinemann.

Herman, J. L., Aschbacher, P. R., & Winters, L. (1992). *A practical guide to alternative assessment.* Alexandria, VA: Association for Supervision and Curriculum Development.

Hill, B. C., & Ruptic, C. (1994). *Practical aspects of authentic assessment: Putting the pieces together.* Norwood, MA: Christopher-Gordon.

Huerta-Macias, A. (1995). Alternative assessment: Responses to commonly asked questions. *TESOL Journal, 5*(1), 8–11.

Illinois content-based exemplars. (1998). Springfield, IL: Illinois State Board of Education.

International Reading Association and National Council of Teachers of English Joint Task Force on Assessment. (1994). *Standards for the assessment of reading and writing.* Newark, DE: Author.

Kamii, C. (Ed.). (1990). *Achievement testing in the early grades: The games grown-ups play.* Washington, DC: National Association for the Education of Young Children.

Kenney, E., & Perry, S. (1994). Talking with parents about performance-based report cards. *Educational Leadership, 52*(2), 24–27.

LaCelle-Peterson, M. W., & Rivera, C. (1994). Is it real for all kids? A framework for equitable assessment policies for English language learners. *Harvard Educational Review, 64* (1), 55–75.

Law, B., & Eckes, M. (1995). *Assessment and ESL: A handbook for K–12 teachers.* Winnipeg, CA: Peguis.

Lazear, D. (1994). *Multiple intelligence approaches to assessment: Solving the assessment conundrum.* Tucson, AZ: Zephyr.

Linder, T. W. (1990). Transdisciplinary play-based assessment. Baltimore, MD: Paul H. Brookes.

Linn, R. L., & Herman, J. L. (1997). *A policymaker's guide to standards-led assessment.* Denver, CO: Education Commission of the States and National Center for Research on Evaluation, Standards, and Student Testing.

Madaus, G. F., & Kellaghan, T. (1993, February). The British experience with "authentic" testing. *Phi Delta Kappan*, 458–469.

Maeroff, G. I. (1991, December). Assessing alternative assessment. *Phi Delta Kappan*, 274–281.

Marzano, R. J., & J. S. Kendall. (1996). *Designing standards-based districts, schools, & classrooms.* Aurora, CO: Mid-Continent Regional Educational Laboratory.

Marzano, R. J., Pickering, D., & McTighe, J. (1993). *Assessing student outcomes.* Alexandria, VA: Association for Supervision and Curriculum Development.

McDonald, J. P. (1993, February). Three pictures of an exhibition: Warm, cool, and hard. *Phi Delta Kappan*, 480–485.

McDonald, J. P., Smith, S., Turner, D., Finney, M., & Barton, E. (1993). *Graduation by exhibition: Assessing genuine achievement.* Alexandria, VA: Association for Supervision and Curriculum Development.

McNamara, M. J., & Deane, D. (1995). Self-assessment activities: Toward autonomy in language learning. *TESOL Journal, 5*(1), 17–21.

National Commission on Testing and Public Policy. (1977). *From gatekeeper to gateway: Transforming testing in America.* Chestnut Hill, MA: Boston College.

National Forum on Assessment. (1995). *Principles and indicators for student assessment systems.* Cambridge, MA: FairTest.

National Research Council. (1996). *National science education standards.* Washington, DC: National Academy Press.

Navarrete, C., Wilde, J., Nelson, C., Martinez, P., & Hargett, G. (1990). *Informal assessment in educational evaluation: Implications for bilingual education programs* (NCBE Program Information Guide Series, 3). Washington, DC: National Clearinghouse for Bilingual Education.

Neill, M., Bursh, P., Schaeffer, B. Thall, C., Yohe, M., & Zappardino, P. (1995). *Implementing performance assessments: A guide to classroom, school, and system reform.* Cambridge, MA: FairTest.

Newmann, F. M., Secada, W. G., & Wehlage, G. G. (1995). *A guide to authentic instruction and assessment: Vision, standards and scoring.* Madison, WI: Wisconsin Center for Education Research.

O'Malley, J. M., & Valdez Pierce, L. (1996). *Authentic assessment for English language learners: Practical approaches for teachers.* Reading, MA: Addison-Wesley.

Popham, W. J. (1993, February). Circumventing the high costs of authentic assessment. *Phi Delta Kappan*, 470–473.

Report of the task force on testing standards to the International Language Testing Association. (1995, September). Victoria, Australia: International Language Testing Association.

Rhodes, L. K. (Ed.). (1993). *Literacy assessment: A handbook of instruments.* Portsmouth, NH: Heinemann.

Ryan, C. D. (1994). *Authentic assessment.* Westminster, CA: Teacher Created Materials.

Seeley, M. M. (1994). The mismatch between assessment and grading. *Educational Leadership, 52*(2), 4–6.

Shepard, L. A. (1989). Why we need better assessments. *Educational Leadership, 46*(7), 4–9.

Sperling, D. H. (1994). Assessment and reporting: A natural pair. *Educational Leadership, 52*(2), 10–13.

TESOL. (1997). *ESL standards for pre-K–12 students.* Alexandria, VA: Author.

TESOL. (1998). *Managing the assessment process: A framework for measuring student attainment of the ESL standards (MAP)* (Professional Paper 5). Alexandria, VA: Author.

Valdez Pierce, L., & O'Malley, J. M. (1992). *Portfolio assessment for language minority students.* Washington, DC: National Clearinghouse for Bilingual Education.

What is authentic evaluation? (1990, Winter). *Fair Test Examiner,* pp. 8–9.

Wiggins, G. P. (1989). Teaching to the (authentic) test. *Educational Leadership, 46*(7), 41–49.

Wiggins, G. P. (1993). *Assessing student performance.* San Francisco, CA: Jossey-Bass.

Worthen, B. R. (1993, February). Critical issues that will determine the future of alternative assessment. *Phi Delta Kappan,* 444–454.

Web Sites

Center for Applied Linguistics: ESL Standards for Pre-K–12 Students (http://www.cal.org/public/ESLStds).

CRESST: National Center for Research on Evaluation, Standards, and Student Testing (http://cresst96.cse.ucla.edu).

FairTest: The National Center for Fair & Open Testing (http://www.fairtest.org).

National Clearinghouse for Bilingual Education (http://www.ncbe.gwu.edu).

Teachers of English to Speakers of Other Languages (http://www.tesol.org).

Also Available From TESOL

*American Quilt: A Reference Book
on American Culture*
Irina Zhukova and Maria Lebedko

Bilingual Education
Donna Christian and Fred Genesee, Editors

*Common Threads of Practice:
Teaching English to Children Around the World*
Katharine Davies Samway and Denise McKeon, Editors

ESL Standards for Pre-K–12 Students
TESOL

Implementing the ESL Standards for Pre-K–12 Students Through Teacher Education
Marguerite Ann Snow, Editor

Integrating the ESL Standards Into Classroom Practice: Grades Pre-K–2
Betty Ansin Smallwood, Editor

Integrating the ESL Standards Into Classroom Practice: Grades 3–5
Katharine Davies Samway, Editor

Integrating the ESL Standards Into Classroom Practice: Grades 6–8
Suzanne Irujo, Editor

Integrating the ESL Standards Into Classroom Practice: Grades 9–12
Barbara Agor, Editor

Managing ESL Programs in Rural and Small Urban Schools
Barney Bérubé

New Ways in Teaching English at the Secondary Level
Deborah J. Short, Editor

New Ways in Teaching Young Children
Linda Schinke-Llano and Rebecca Rauff, Editors

New Ways in Using Authentic Materials in the Classroom
Ruth E. Larimer and Leigh Schleicher, Editors

New Ways in Using Communicative Games in Language Teaching
Nikhat Shameem and Makhan Tickoo, Editors

New Ways of Classroom Assessment
James Dean Brown, Editor

Reading and Writing in More Than One Language:
Lessons for Teachers
Elizabeth Franklin, Editor

Teacher Education
Karen E. Johnson, Editor

Teaching in Action: Case Studies From Second Language Classrooms
Jack C. Richards, Editor

Training Others to Use the ESL Standards:
A Professional Developmental Manual
Deborah J. Short, Emily L. Gómez, Nancy Cloud, Anne Katz,
Margo Gottlieb, Margaret Malone

For more information, contact
Teachers of English to Speakers of Other Languages, Inc.
700 South Washington Street, Suite 200
Alexandria, Virginia 22314 USA
Tel 703-836-0774 • Fax 703-836-6447 • publications@tesol.org • http://www.tesol.org/